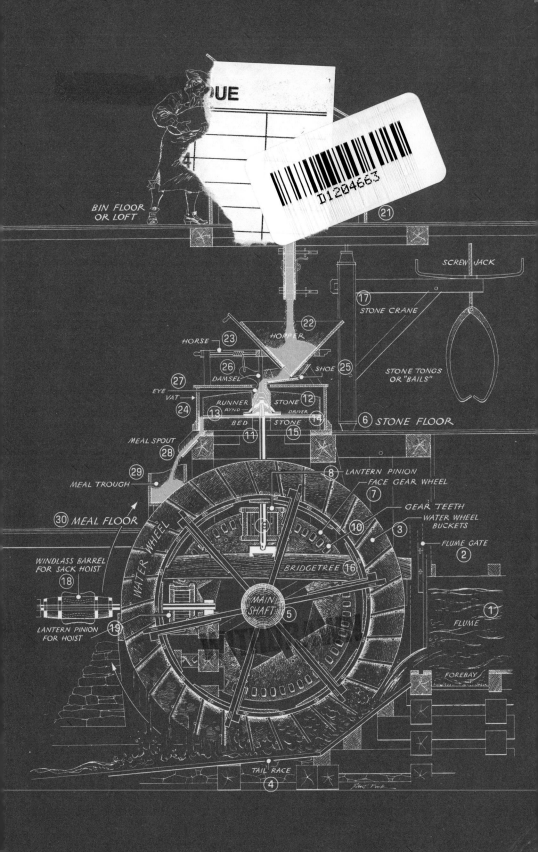

THE MILL
At Philipsburg Manor
Upper Mills
and
A Brief History of
Milling

PHILIPSBURG MANOR, UPPER MILLS

The gristmill and Manor House on the Pocantico River in
North Tarrytown, New York, formed the core of the
commercial trading complex which served as the northern
headquarters of the approximately 50,000 acres originally
encompassed by Philipsburg Manor. Today, the operating
gristmill and restored Manor House, maintained by Sleepy
Hollow Restorations, appear much as they would have in
the late seventeenth and early eighteenth centuries.

THE MILL
At Philipsburg Manor
Upper Mills
and
A Brief History of
Milling

by
CHARLES HOWELL
and
ALLAN KELLER

with a Foreword by
Rex Wailes

SLEEPY HOLLOW RESTORATIONS
Tarrytown · New York

All illustrations except as otherwise noted are from the collections of Sleepy Hollow Restorations.

Library of Congress Cataloging in Publication Data
Howell, Charles, 1926–
The mill at Philipsburg Manor, Upper Mills
and a brief history of milling.
Bibliography: p.
Includes index.
1. Flour-mills—New York (State)—North Tarrytown—History.
2. Grain—Milling—History.
3. North Tarrytown, N.Y.—Industries.
I. Keller, Allan, joint author.
TS2135.U62N73 1977   664'.72'09747'277   75-7156
ISBN 0-912882-22-0

For information, address the publisher:
Sleepy Hollow Restorations, Inc.
Tarrytown, New York 10591

ISBN 0-912882-22-0

Library of Congress Catalog Card Number: 75-7156

First Printing

Printed in the United States of America

DESIGNED BY RAY FREIMAN

Table of Contents

List of Illustrations

Foreword

by Rex Wailes

It was in 1923 when I was training as a Mechanical Engineer that I first became interested in windmills from the historical, aesthetic and mechanical points of view. At that time there were about 350 windmills left at work in England. In spare time and vacations I continued to visit mills, millers and millwrights and by 1926 had systematized a recording of data and was taking interior photographs with a wide angle lens and artificial light. In 1929 I met William Sumner Appleton, of Boston, the founder of the Society for the Preservation of New England Antiquities, and with encouragement from him I visited and recorded mills on Nantucket, Rhode Island and Cape Cod, at the same time gathering historical data. Later, in 1932, I visited Eastern Long Island and with the help of the millwright Felix Dominy recorded the accessible windmills in that area.

In 1929 on returning to England I found that the London-based Society for the Protection of Ancient Buildings, founded in 1877, had just organized a Windmill Committee and I was invited to join it as

11

Honorary Technical Advisor, visiting windmills in my
spare time up and down the country, preparing re-
ports, obtaining estimates from millwrights and check-
ing work done to specifications. During the remaining
years before World War II, I undertook a survey of the
remaining British tide mills and was able to visit
windmills in France, Germany and Spain, and after the
war in the Netherlands, France, Sweden and Bar-
bados, and both wind and watermills in Portugal,
Denmark and Finland. I was also able to provide Colonial Williamsburg with drawings from which their mill
was reconstructed.

At the end of World War II only about 50 windmills
were left in England and I was able to turn to recording
watermills. From 1963 I was appointed First Consul-
tant to the Industrial Monuments Survey of Britain
and was instructed that in addition to recording all
types of industrial monuments, watermills included, I
should pay especial attention to a single subject of my
own choosing. I chose the water-driven mills used for
grinding stone for pottery as these are going out of use
rapidly. The earliest examples were in Staffordshire,
and it was there that I met Charles Howell who became
my guide, philosopher and friend whenever I was in
that county or adjoining areas. His wide knowledge of
the location and the history of watermills, steam power
and virtually all aspects of industrial monuments as
well as his attractive friendly personality, made him the
ideal companion on the Survey.

The particular Survey of the grinding mills in Staffordshire resulted incidentally in the preservation in
running order of one such mill at Cheddleton. This

was through the remarkable enthusiasm, energy and tact of Mr. Robert Copeland of Spode Limited who formed a Preservation Trust for the purpose. The result has been highly successful and both Mr. Howell and myself are among the Trustees.

I was very fortunate in being able to accept an invitation to visit North Tarrytown and the three properties belonging to Sleepy Hollow Restorations in the Fall of 1973. Not all was entirely strange to me as I had twice seen the film, "The Mill at Philipsburg Manor," which shows both the mill and her miller, Charles Howell, at work. What I was not prepared for was the atmosphere that has been created, recalling so clearly a life in times past; nor had I realized the actual situation of the mill half a mile up from the Hudson on the Pocantico River, extremely convenient for import and export of goods and produce. The railway has now blocked the river below the mill pond but there is still a rise and fall of three feet in the head due to the tide, so that the mill can in some sense be considered a semi-tidal mill. Moreover the whole atmosphere of the mill is authentic even down to the traditional control of rodents in the mill by cats, particularly Dusty, who could in truth be described as Mr. Howell's "little personal cat," running along the handrail of the bridge beside him and waiting for him to come home whatever the weather.

It is very fitting that the mill should be so fortunate as to have such a miller as Charles Howell. Not only is he a highly qualified grain miller and a skilled stone dresser, he is also a fine craftsman and millwright, has read widely and deeply on the subject of mills and has an exceedingly retentive memory. He has a long background of practical experience and gives advice with admirable clarity to all who consult him, appreciating as he does the points of view of both miller and millwright. In addition he has the ability to explain clearly the working of the mill, not only to young people to whom a mill is a novelty, but also to those who are well versed in that which was in old times called "the mechanick arts." And his clarity extends to writing on the subject as this book shows.

Readers of this book will find that it is far more than what is implied by its title. Not only is it a history of the mill at Philipsburg Manor, Upper Mills, but it includes also an historical background which explains why the mill was rebuilt and how it is operated, all with the aid of a generous number of illustrations. It also includes the story of grain-milling in America as well as the methods of harnessing natural sources of power. The processes of milling and maintaining a mill are all clearly explained both in text and illustrations.

The story of the rebirth of the mill is as fascinating as its history and by the time that the end of the book is reached one can only marvel at the ingenuity and resourcefulness shown by those who had to turn the vision of reconstruction into reality. At the close one feels a profound sense of gratitude to those who had the vision to conceive the project and enabled it to be carried through so that all who wish can see a working mill in its beautiful historical setting.

REX WAILES
Beaconsfield, Bucks, England

Early History

At some time after the dawn of civilization, the first hunters learned that they could augment their diet by gathering certain wild foods to go with the meat they killed. Next they discovered that if they planted the seeds of these wild foods they could harvest them more easily and store them more safely against the time when wild game might be hard to capture.

There was a catch in this forward step. Cereals, in raw form, were virtually inedible. So the first cave man who used two stones to smash the grains was no small benefactor in his era. Improvements—which probably consumed centuries—brought about the first crude type of mill, what we know as the mortar and pestle.

A stone with a depression in it held the grain while another stone, shaped like a club, was used to strike the cereal. Better than two ordinary rocks, it still required great strength and patience to pulverize the kernels into meal. Some tribes developed a variant of the mortar and pestle in which the grain was ground between a saddle-shaped stone and one not unlike today's rolling pin. This saddle-stone mill was improved by adding levers to use the full weight of the miller's body and enlarging the surface and abrasiveness of the stones.

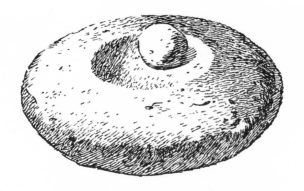

EARLY MILLING DEVICES

The earliest method of grinding cereal grains was probably simply to crush them between two stones; an example of such an early milling device (top) was found in a cave in the valley of Vézère, France, and is believed to date from about 25,000 years ago. Refinements of this technique produced the mortar and pestle (bottom, left) and the saddle-stone mill (bottom, right). Drawings by Robert Fink.

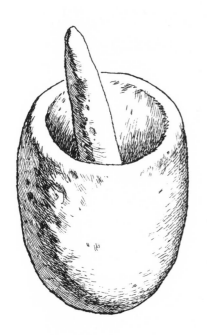

MORTAR AND PESTLE
The mortar and pestle, one of the earliest forms of milling devices, remained in common use for many centuries. Shown here is a large wooden mortar and pestle in use at Philipsburg Manor, Upper Mills.

An obvious next step involved cutting grooves in the rubbing stone and base stone so that the grooves crossed each other and provided a shearing action. It was the beginning of the technique that was to become common with powered mills. Grooved, or dressed, stones did a much better job of grinding the grain into a smooth meal.

Advances in milling varied with different civilizations, reflecting the degree of technology in them. Certain tribes in backward lands never went beyond the mortar and pestle or the saddle-stone mills. When the first white men arrived in the New World the Indians were still using the former and in some remote areas of Brazil and other countries the saddle-stone mill is still in use today.

Along the shores of the Mediterranean, as culture flowered in the millennium before Christ, rotary motion came into use, crude at first, but full of promise. Probably the first version consisted of two circular flat stones, the top turned by hand against the stationary bottom one. Step by step it was improved upon until the top, or runner, stone was made with a hole in the center. Through this opening extended a spindle on which the upper stone rested by means of a bearing called a rynd. The grain to be milled was hand fed through this hole. As the runner stone turned against the nonmoving bottom stone the grain was milled exactly as it is today by millstones in a gristmill. Eventually a stick or lever was fastened to one side of the runner stone so the miller could turn the wheel easily.

This hand-powered mill, called a quern, spread throughout Europe and most of the rest of the world, remaining in use, in some isolated areas, even to this

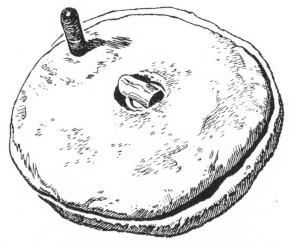

QUERN

Rotary motion was used to grind grain in a quern (above), another early form of mill consisting of two circular flat stones, the upper rotated upon the lower stationary stone. A working example of a quern (below) may be seen today in the gristmill at Philipsburg Manor, Upper Mills. Drawing by Robert Fink.

day. As late as the last century there was an attempt to keep Scottish cotters from using querns, apparently in an effort to force them to buy meal on which a tax could be levied.

The quern was a great advance. It showed how two stones, one of them moving in a circular manner, could do a better job of milling and with less expenditure of muscle than any previous form of mill. Within a short time improvements were made, leading to the use of animal power to turn larger quernlike mills and to the designing of a better mill using the same idea.

This latter development, believed to date from about two centuries B.C., was perfected by the Romans. Known as the conical quern or hourglass mill, it used a conical-shaped lower stone and an upper stone cut to fit rather closely over the stationary one. The top portion of the upper stone was hopper-shaped. Through the center of the top stone, which was fitted in place with a metal plate, or rynd, that turned on a spindle extending through the lower stone, the grain was fed by gravity between the grinding surfaces.

Power was exerted by means of bars or handles fastened to the perimeter of the upper stone. The miller, alone or with help from assistants, walked around the device, turning the runner stone, rather like a capstan. Later horses and donkeys were substituted for the men.

As with the quern, this mill did not work with the two stones in actual contact. The upper stone rested on a spindle extending through the bottom one so that, in fact, there was about a sixteenth of an inch of space between the abrasive surfaces. By allowing the spindle

HORSE-DRIVEN MILL
Animal power (right top) was sometimes used to drive mills.

CONICAL QUERN

An improved version of the quern (below), called a conical
quern or hourglass mill, employed a conical-shaped lower
stone and an upper stone cut to fit over the lower stone.
Grain was fed between the stones from the hopper-shaped
top portion of the upper stone. Photo: National Museum of
History and Technology, Smithsonian Institution.

to rest in a socket beneath the bottom stone which in turn was borne by a timber that could be raised or lowered, the distance between the grinding faces could be altered at the miller's desire to produce fine or coarse meal. This leverlike timber is still used in varying forms and is known as the bridgetree.

Archaeologists excavating the ruins of Pompeii, which was destroyed in the eruption of Vesuvius in A.D. 79, discovered several fairly large mills of the hourglass type. Others of large and small size have been turned up at other locations around the world.

So far, power had been supplied by man or beasts of burden. The latter made life easier for the miller but the process was still slow and inefficient. Centuries went by with small change until the Greeks turned to water for power. First mentioned around 85 B.C., these early watermills were exceedingly simple in their engineering. The spindle on which the top stone rested passed through a hole in the bottom or bed stone and extended far enough for blades to be attached. Water directed against these blades turned the upper stone without requiring any gearing.

The first waterpowered mill was known as both the "Greek" and the "Norse" mill and, as if this were not confusing enough, there is some evidence indicating that it did not originate in either Greece or Scandinavia but rather in Asia Minor. Nonetheless it showed that men were seeking a better source of power and had turned to water with considerable success.

A few years ago, scuba divers operating off the north coast of the island of Cyprus, near the city of Kyrenia, discovered the remains of an early wood sail-

HORIZONTAL WATERMILL

The horizontal watermill dates back to Greek and Roman times, yet this type of mill can still be seen in daily use in parts of Portugal and Spain and in many Latin American countries. The horizontal mill shown above is located in Lemiro Carvide, Portugal. Below is a horizontal mill wheel from Alcobaca, Portugal, about 46 cm. in diameter, bonded with iron. This wheel, of the "Greek" type found in warmer climates, has spoon-shaped blades. The blades of the "Norse" type wheel were straight and inclined at an angle to facilitate ice removal. Photos: Rex Wailes.

ing vessel on the bottom, covered and surrounded by scores of huge amphorae, ceramic vases used in Biblical times and before to hold wine and oils.

Experts raised the vessel, which was a single-sailed coastal freighter. Using radioactive carbon, they determined that the vessel had sunk about 300 years before Christ, during the tempestuous reign of Alexander the Great. It is, without any doubt, the oldest vessel recovered from the sea. By knowledge of ancient trade routes and commerce the experts were able to fix the vessel's probable course on its last voyage. They believe most of the wine was loaded at Samos, with a smaller portion taken on board at Rhodes.

What is of greatest interest to readers of this account is the fact that several millstones were also recovered from where they had lain for more than two millennia beneath the Mediterranean. These stones, the experts have reason to believe, were loaded aboard the freighter at the island of Kos and were probably for querns, or possibly for early horizontal mills.

The Romans studied the Greek mill with its power passing directly from a horizontal water wheel to a vertical drive shaft without gears, and probably improved it before going on to another type altogether.

The horizontal mill was easy to construct and operate, and was efficient enough for small family or communal purposes. Made almost entirely of wood, it consisted of a hub into which were morticed a number of blades or vanes. The shaft on which the hub was fastened passed up through a hole in the bottom stone—where there was a crude wooden bearing—and was fastened to the runner stone. When water was directed from the millstream through a chute or inclined trough against the vanes or blades it turned the water wheel, which of course made the upper stone revolve. Below the water wheel with its blades was a simple thrust bearing on which turned the bottom end of the shaft. This bearing, like the one on the hourglass mill, was placed on a bridgetree which the miller could use to raise or lower the upper stone.

Grain was fed into this mill from a box hopper above the runner stone through a tapering wooden trough called a "shoe." The shoe was constantly vibrated by one of various types of eccentric devices to keep the grain flowing.

Such mills were used by early settlers in America on the Atlantic coast and there are others in the far west showing that Spanish conquerors of Mexico and California carried the Norse or Greek mill into that territory during their explorations.

Travelers who get off the beaten path in Spain, Portugal, and many Latin American countries can still see this type of mill in daily use. It was improved here and there, as when the water wheel was enclosed to its full depth in a tublike enclosure to keep the water from escaping before it had delivered its full thrust, but the tub mill, as it was called, was only a variation of the horizontal mill: an improvement, not a new form.

While the main effort of the inventors moved from quern to hourglass mill to horizontal mill, other forms of mills were used with varying success. They were less important than those variants that led to the familiar structures along the streams of the world, but they had their place.

TUB MILL

The tub mill was a variation of the horizontal watermill in which the water wheel was enclosed to its full depth in a tublike enclosure in order to prevent water from escaping before it had delivered its full thrust. The photo above, taken prior to restoration, shows the shaft of an early American tub wheel at the Southside Sportsmen's Club, Connetquot River State Park, Oakdale, Long Island. Below is a reconstructed tub wheel at Old Sturbridge Village, Sturbridge, Mass. Photo by Donald F. Eaton.

The best known was the plumping mill which grew out of men's desire to utilize the mortar and pestle idea without breaking their backs. At first they let a sapling do most of the work. They built a mortar out of a hardwood tree trunk. Then they fastened a smaller piece of wood to the top of the sapling. The grain was placed in the hollow container and the "hammer" was rammed down upon it, crushing it into flour. The resiliency of the sapling lifted the hammer up again, cutting down on the miller's work. Up and down went the hammer and, in time, a coarse meal was obtained from the grain. This early plumping mill, also called a sapling mill, was particularly popular in the interior of the South where water power was not readily available.

Realizing that the sapling took only half of the burden, early inventors figured out a way to make water do it all. They substituted a sweep for the sapling, fastening a box to one end of the sweep and a hardwood pestle to the opposite. Water was directed from the nearest source by means of a hollow reed or wooden trough. As soon as the box filled with water it became heavier than the pestle and forced the sweep down at its end. As it fell the box emptied itself, whereupon the pestle end fell in its turn into a hollowed tree trunk or other similar mortarlike receptacle in which the grain to be ground had been placed.

As the box filled and then tipped itself, emptying the water, the sweep moved up and down ceaselessly, with no need for the householder to pay more than a little attention to the milling process. The endless, repetitive thumping of the pestle into the hollowed

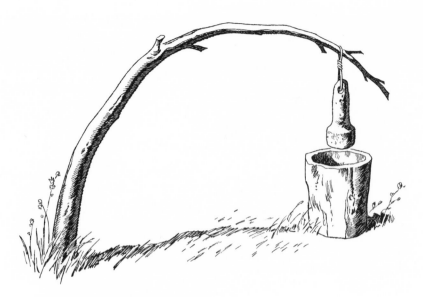

SAPLING AND PLUMPING MILL
The sapling mill shown above was an early form of plumping mill which harnessed the resiliency of a sapling to aid in driving a mortar and pestle. Another type of plumping mill harnessed the flow of water into and out of a receptacle to drive a mortar and pestle. Drawings by Robert Fink.

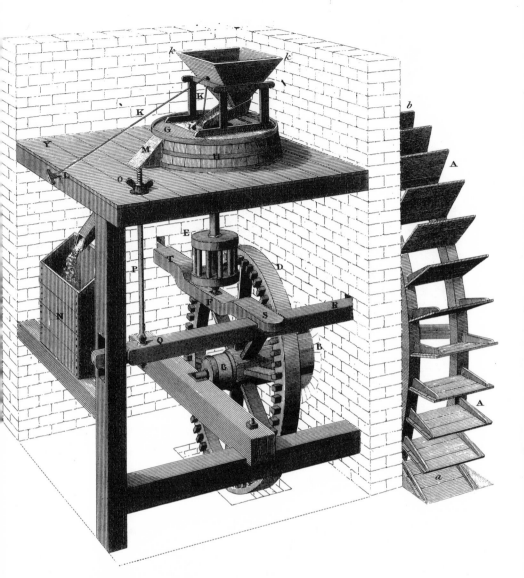

VITRUVIAN WATERMILL

The earliest known description of a vertical watermill is found in the writings of Vitruvius, a Roman engineer. The watermill shown in this illustration is of the type designed by Vitruvius. Drawing courtesy of National Museum of History and Technology, Smithsonian Institution.

tree trunk echoed across the fields and from hillside to hillside. Many a traveler in the early days may have known he was approaching a home or settlement in the wilderness by hearing a plumping mill in the distance.

In the years immediately preceding the Christian era, the Romans had made great strides carrying water long distances by aqueducts and mastering other hydraulic arts. They knew something about the removal of sewage by a steady flow of water and they naturally understood the crude dynamics of water power actuated by gravity. They had adopted the horizontal mill from Greeks but were dissatisfied with its degree of efficiency.

So far as is known now, the first mention of the vertical mill, similar to the many that helped feed colonial America and that still exist in scattered locations, is found in the writings of one Vitruvius, a Roman engineer. He described the new type of mill in documents made public between the years 20 and 11 B.C.

This type of mill involved a vertical water wheel fastened to a horizontal drive shaft. To carry the power to the millstones, gears were used, changing the direction of the drive 90 degrees. In later developments, this gearing also increased the speed of the spindle on which the runner stone was supported, in ratios determined by individual millers. The type of mill design described by Vitruvius endured as one of the most common for centuries to come.

Milling Comes to America

From the time of Vitruvius to the arrival of the first settlers in North America the concept of the vertical mill changed very little. There were small improvements, of course, but the main idea remained much the same, regardless of where these mills were operated. The first white men to step ashore in North America must have marveled at two things: the existence of plenty of timber and the presence of countless swift streams and creeks in which there was an ample supply of water tumbling downhill. They realized at once that mills would be easy to build and, except in the north, could operate virtually all year.

Although it is impossible to determine precisely how many mills existed in North America during the seventeenth and eighteenth centuries, they must have totaled somewhere in the thousands. There were few hamlets without a mill and many had more than one to perform varying chores. A small stream near New Preston, Connecticut, for instance, supplied the power in the early days for nearly thirty mills. Most were gristmills; but others pressed apples for cider or linseed for oil, sawed wood, made plaster, and performed other tasks.

The horizontal mill survived here and there along with its heir, the tub mill, until modern times, but the mill that supplied the staff of life to the developing nation was the vertical variety, standing by a millpond, its great wheel splashing and dripping, its solid oak shaft carrying the power to one or two pairs of stones inside.

These water wheels were of four main types—(1) overshot; (2) pitchback; (3) breastshot or breast (low, middle, or high); and (4) undershot—the names indicating the point on the wheel at which the water was fed to it. If the wheel is regarded as a clock face, with the water coming to it from the left, then the overshot wheel is fed at about 12:30 or 1:00 o'clock, the pitchback at about 11:00 or 11:30, the breastshot at between 8:00 and 10:30, and the undershot at about 7:00 o'clock. In these examples, with the water coming in from the left, the overshot would revolve clockwise, and the three other types counterclockwise.

Throughout the colonial period these vertical water wheels were almost completely built of wood, with five main parts: (1) the shaft, (2) the arms, (3) the shrouding or rims, (4) the sole or drum boards, and (5) the partitions which formed the buckets or floats. The shafts were almost universally of oak, those used in gristmills usually being from 18 to 24 inches in diameter, dressed in a circular, polygonal, or square form, and fitted with iron bands around them. In the ends of the shafts iron gudgeons were inserted, so that the protruding ends of the gudgeons ran on the bearings, which were often of stone, though wood and brass were also used. In some cases water was used to lubri-

WATERMILL SHAFT
The main shaft in a watermill was almost always made of oak, often from the trunk of a single tree. Shown here is a shaft uncovered during archaeological excavations at Philipsburg Manor, Upper Mills.

MILL SHAFT AND GUDGEON

The end of the mill shaft was fitted with iron bands. Into the end of the shaft was inserted an iron gudgeon, which ran on bearings of stone, wood, or brass. Miller Charles Howell is here shown at work on repairs to the shaft of the mill at Philipsburg Manor. The wooden wedges placed around the gudgeon to insure a tight fit would be trimmed flush with the end of the shaft before operation. Repairs of this sort were necessary at five to ten year intervals on most watermills.

cate the stone bearing, particularly on the outside bearing of a water wheel. A small wooden spout conducted a trickle of water on to the revolving gudgeon to give constant lubrication; rendered animal fats were also used as lubrication on all these types of early bearings. The type of wheel used depended on the head or fall of water available and on the mill site in general. Most of the wheels were designed by the skilled millwrights who built them. The majority of early colonial water wheels were comparatively small in diameter, often between 10 and 15 feet. Later colonial wheels were much larger and more powerful.

Overshot wheels were employed at most heads of water over 10 feet high. The water was conveyed to the top of the wheel by a wooden trough or flume and fed into the buckets. These buckets were formed by boards set at an angle toward the stream, and the ends of the boards were set into slots in the shrouds or rims of the wheel. The depth of the shrouds varied, but was usually 9 to 15 inches. The bottom edges of the buckets were fastened to the sole or drum formed by planks secured to the inside edge of the shrouds. Wheels of this type of construction were often referred to as "bucket wheels." Power generated by overshot wheels depends almost entirely on the weight of water in the buckets, but the forward momentum of the water as it enters the buckets adds a slight increment to their power.

A variation to the overshot water wheel was the pitchback wheel, in which the water was conveyed to the top, or almost to the top, of the wheel by a flume. The buckets in the pitchback were set at an angle

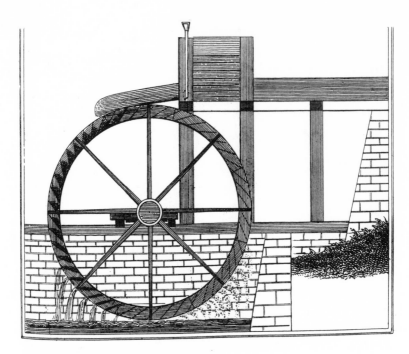

OVERSHOT WHEEL

An overshot wheel is powered by a head of water striking the wheel just forward of its highest point. This illustration of an overshot wheel is taken from Oliver Evans's *The Young Mill-wright and Miller's Guide* (Philadelphia, 1795).

OVERSHOT WHEELS

Examples of overshot water wheels may still be found today in New York State. Above is the Rest Place Mill at High Falls, in Ulster County, near New Paltz, N.Y. (photo: Charles Howell). Below is an overshot wheel at Stony Brook, Long Island (photo: Rex Wailes).

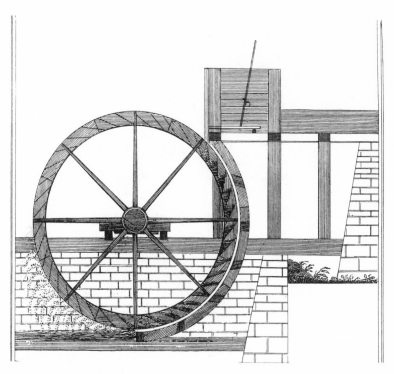

PITCHBACK WHEEL

In the pitchback wheel, water strikes the wheel at or just back of its highest point; the wheel in this illustration by Oliver Evans would revolve in a clockwise direction.

opposite to those in an overshot. The end of the flume
and the control gate or "shut" were adapted so that the
water fed downward into the buckets at the reverse
direction to the flow of the stream, causing the pitchback wheel to revolve in the opposite direction. Behind
the wheel was an arc of stone or wood, known as an
apron, usually of the same radius as the wheel. The
edge of the buckets ran close to this apron, to confine
the water and prevent it from spilling from the buckets
before arriving at the lowest point of the fall. An
efficient type of apron would terminate with a step
downward of about 6 inches, usually about a foot before the lowest point of the run. This enabled the
water to be discharged rapidly from the buckets, so as
not to impede the upward motion of the wheel. Like
overshot wheels, pitchbacks derived most of their
power from the weight of the water in the buckets, but
they received a certain amount of additional impulse
from the water as it fed in from the flume.

Breastshot water wheels, most commonly used at
falls of between 6 and 10 feet, were of construction
similar to overshot and pitchback wheels, and aprons
were usually fitted to retain the water in the same type
of enclosed buckets as in the case of the pitchbacks.

In middle and low breastshot wheels, the buckets
were deeper, to deal with the increased volume of
water required for the low head of water to develop
power equivalent to that obtained by a high breastshot
wheel. Breastshot wheels combined both the weight
and impulse of the water for their operation, and
well-designed wheels of this type were very popular.

For low falls of water undershot wheels were
employed. These wheels were moved entirely by the

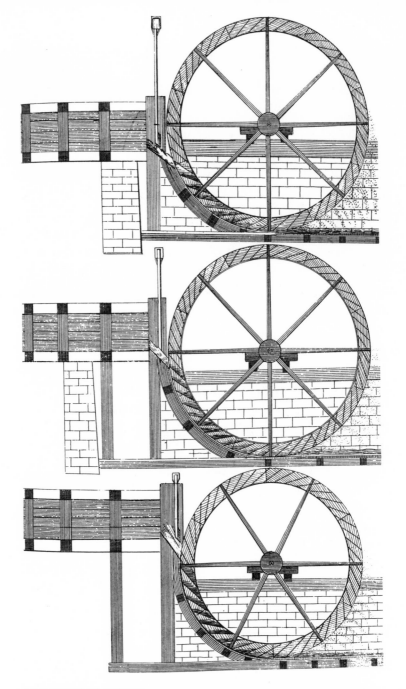

BREASTSHOT WHEEL
These Oliver Evans drawings represent three types of
breastshot wheels—from top to bottom, a low, middle, and
high wheel. According to Evans, "Breast wheels differ but
little in their structure or material from overshot, excepting
only that the water passes under instead of over them and
they must be wider in proportion as their fall is less."

BREASTSHOT WHEEL AT OLD STURBRIDGE VILLAGE
This breastshot water wheel, shown here covered by falling
snow, is on the mill at Old Sturbridge Village,
Massachusetts. Photo by Donald F. Eaton.

impulse of the water and consequently required much greater quantities of water to produce the same power as developed by the overshot, pitchback, or breastshot wheels. In construction the undershot wheels differed little from the bucket-type wheels, except that the buckets were replaced by radial floats. The early undershot wheels usually had floats constructed of flat boards with no right-angle back or sole boards on the inside rim of the wheel, but some later wheels increased efficiency by having these backs fitted to prevent the water from shooting over the floats. In some undershot wheels the floats were fitted into slots in deep shrouds or rims; in others the rims were not so deep but were of thicker timber, which was morticed and had short protruding arms or "starts" driven into them, to which the floats were fastened. Water was admitted to undershot wheels by a sluice gate, called a "shut." At its base this would be set as close as possible to the wheel, on such an angle that its top moved away from the wheel; in this way the shut acted as a conductor, guiding the water in a downward path to strike the floats in the operative direction of the wheel. Undershot wheels ran in an enclosed channel, which in early colonial mills was built of either wood or stone. The base of the channel formed a close-fitting apron as in the case of the pitchback and breastshot wheels. Ordinarily undershot wheels were built from about 10 to 25 feet in diameter. The floats were from 14 to 16 inches apart at the circumference and about 12 to 28 inches in depth.

The relative efficiency of the various types of water wheels was long a matter of speculation and

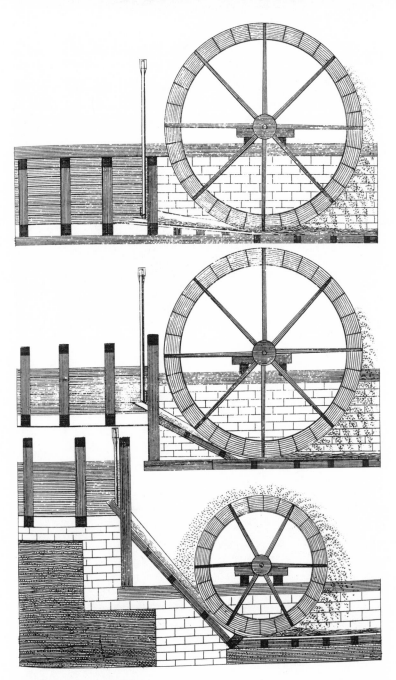

UNDERSHOT WHEEL

In an undershot wheel, water strikes the wheel near the bottom of the wheel, as in these Oliver Evans drawings.

SLUICE GATE

The flow of water from the headrace or millpond into the
flume, and from the flume to the water wheel, could be
controlled by the use of a sluice gate (also variously called a
flume gate, control gate, or shut). The photo above shows
the sluice gate at the millpond end of the flume at
Philipsburg Manor, Upper Mills. Below is a detail of the
closed sluice gate, with no water in the flume.

controversy; but, of course, the efficiency of all the wheels depended on the head of water available, that is, the difference in level between the water feeding the wheel (the "head" water) and that leaving it (the "tail" water). The greater the head of water, the larger the wheel could be and the more numerous the buckets. The overshot and pitchback wheels needed the greatest head of water and were the most efficient, for a larger number of buckets were filled at one time. For the same reasons a high breastshot wheel was more efficient than a middle or low breast wheel and the middle and low breast wheels were more efficient than the undershot wheels.

The water that supplied the power to the wheel could be troublesome as well as helpful. For maximum efficiency the tail water had to leave the area as swiftly as possible. One way to arrange for this was to build a free-flowing tailrace laid in the direction of the stream so that the water from the wheel could rejoin the stream without appreciable obstruction. These tailraces were built of both wood and stone, depending on which material was closer at hand.

Various kinds of timber were used for the water wheels. Some were made completely of oak, others had an oak shaft but arms, soling, and buckets made from other kinds of timber. Pine of certain types was found to be fairly long-lasting in water wheels, but cypress was perhaps the best rot-resisting wood discovered for water wheel construction. Although wooden water wheels were always strongly made, exposure to water, ice, snow, and sun shortened the active life of the wood and repairs were frequently necessary. In a period of five to ten years, almost every

TAILRACE

When the water wheel is in operation, water leaving the wheel, called tail water, flows out through the tailrace, visible here as a region of white, frothy water. Miller Charles Howell is seen explaining the water wheel to a visitor at Philipsburg Manor, Upper Mills.

part of a wooden wheel, except the main shaft, would have to be repaired or replaced.

Some of the early mills were erected on natural waterfalls; but at most mill sites it was essential to build a dam to obtain the necessary head of water. To withstand the considerable pressure of the water, the dams and weirs had to be solidly constructed. Some consisted of continuous stone-filled cribbing of rough-hewn oak, pine, or locust logs, which were usually more than 9 inches square with each piece notched into those above and below. This cribbing supported a series of strongbacks, spaced about 4 feet 6 inches apart, of both rough and hewn logs mostly around 10 inches in diameter. These strongbacks were laid parallel to the axis of the stream and at about a 45-degree angle, with the apex upstream and a double thickness of 1-inch planking nailed to them. There were, of course, many different ways of constructing timber dams, and many were constructed of logs and stone combined. Other dams were built completely of rocks or stone, which might be laid dry or with mortar, or perhaps bolted with iron bars.

From the dam to the mill, the water flowed through a headrace, which was sometimes of considerable length. The final channel through which the water flowed before reaching the wheel, the flume or sluiceway, was often of timber construction. Wooden flumes were usually a box section with plank sides and bottom supported on masonry piers, wood cribbing, or piles. The longitudinal members, or "rangers," were notched into the flume sills and the bearers above the piers or piles; all were spiked solidly together.

SAWMILL AT GLENS FALLS
The sawmill at the village of Glens Falls, New York, was
erected on a natural waterfall. This illustration is from
Jacques Milbert's *Picturesque Itinerary of the Hudson River,*
originally published in Paris in 1828–29.

MILL DAM AT PHILIPSBURG MANOR, UPPER MILLS
At most early mill sites, it was essential to build a dam to obtain the necessary head of water. Visitors can see an example of such a dam reconstructed at Philipsburg Manor, Upper Mills.

FLUME
The flume or sluiceway is a channel which carries water from the millpond or headrace to the water wheel. This photo shows the wooden flume at Philipsburg Manor, Upper Mills.

In the early colonial gristmills each water wheel was geared to drive a single pair of stones by one-step gearing. To the water wheel shaft was attached a large face gear which engaged a lantern pinion, often called a wallower. The purpose of the gears was twofold: to transfer the direction of the drive from horizontal to vertical, and to increase the speed of the millstone spindle as opposed to the slower motion of the water wheel shaft. The ratio of the gears varied according to the individual ideas of millwrights, but was often around one to five. A good millwright avoided simple gear ratios by the insertion of a "hunting cog" (e.g., there might be sixty-one cogs in the face wheel and ten in the lantern pinion). This precaution ensured that the same two cogs did not continuously mesh together in a regular pattern, thus avoiding potential uneven wear due to inequalities in the repeatedly meeting cog-faces.

Most of the face gear wheels in the early mills were constructed with two wooden arms passing through mortices in the water wheel shaft to form four spokes. The rims, which were pegged or bolted to the arms, were laminated, the two thicknesses being pinned together with bolts or treenails and arranged so that the grain of the wood crossed at right angles. Each ring of the rim was in four segments known as "cants," the joints of which were staggered so that they came together directly in the center of the cant in the adjoining ring. The cogs were driven into mortices in the sides or faces of the cants, passed through both thicknesses, and were secured in place by pegs or wedges in the shank ends.

FACE GEAR AND LANTERN PINION
In many mills, face gears engaging lantern pinions are used to transfer the direction of the drive from horizontal to vertical and to increase the speed of the millstone spindle relative to the water wheel shaft. These photos show typical examples of a face gear and lantern pinion used in such a fashion. Photos: Rex Wailes.

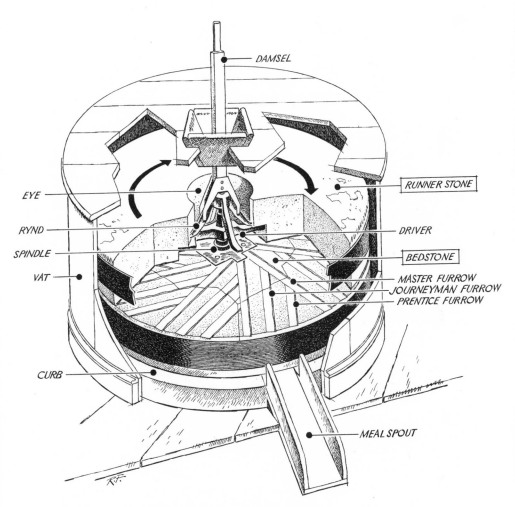

DAMSEL

RUNNER STONE

EYE

RYND

SPINDLE

VAT

DRIVER

BEDSTONE

MASTER FURROW
JOURNEYMAN FURROW
PRENTICE FURROW

CURB

MEAL SPOUT

CUTAWAY DRAWING OF MILLSTONES IN USE
This cutaway drawing shows the grinding action of two
millstones with a right-hand dress. Drawing by Robert Fink.

Water to power the mill is conducted from the mill pond to the water wheel by the flume [1]. The amount of water fed to the wheel is controlled by the flume gate [2]. When the flume gate is raised, water emerges under pressure and strikes the buckets [3] of the water wheel, causing it to revolve. After powering the wheel, water flows away down the tail race [4].

The arms, or spokes, of the water wheel are morticed into the main shaft [5], which transmits the power into the mill building, where the millstones are located on the stone floor [6]. Attached to the main shaft are face gear wheels [7], one directly under each pair of stones. The face gear wheels engage into lantern pinions [8], which are mounted on the millstone spindles [9], thus transferring the drive from horizontal to vertical and also increasing the shaft speed as the larger number of gear teeth [10] in the face gear wheel engage the fewer staves of the lantern pinion.

The millstone spindles pass through the neck bearing [11] in the center of the bedstone. The runner stone [12] is pivoted atop the spindle by a socket bearing called the cockeye in the center of the rynd [13]; the pivot point of the spindle is known as the cock head. Just above the neck bearing is fitted the driver [14], which engages the runner stone and causes it to revolve while the bedstone [15] remains stationary. The millstone spindles are supported by foot-step bearings fitted into bridging boxes mounted on the bridgetree [16], which can be raised or lowered in a process known as tentering.

Next to the millstones is the stone crane [17], used to lift and invert the runner stone. The windlass barrel [18] for the sack hoist is driven by another lantern pinion from one of the face wheels.

Grain in the grain bins [20] on the grain floor [21] flows by gravity into a spout which delivers it into the hopper [22], supported by the horse [23] atop the stone case or vat [24]. The base of the hopper feeds grain into the shoe [25], an inclined tapering wooden trough. The revolving runner stone turns the damsel [26], a square shaft which taps against a block of wood in the shoe, causing it to vibrate and thus feed grain into the eye [27] of the runner stone.

Grain ground between the stones emerges as meal around the periphery of the stones and is trapped in the vat. The runner stone carries meal around to the meal spout [28], where it is discharged into the meal trough [29] on the meal floor [30] where it is put into sacks or barrels for delivery or bolting.

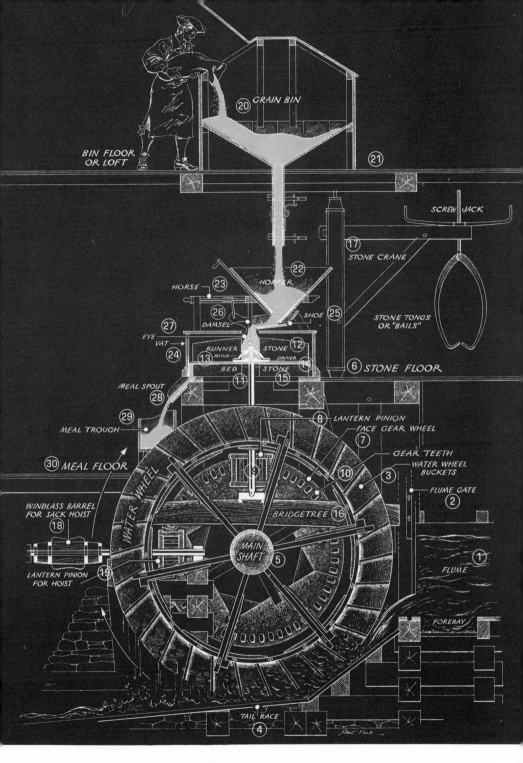

CROSS-SECTION OF GRISTMILL
This drawing by Robert Fink is based upon the
reconstructed water mill at Philipsburg Manor,
Upper Mills.

Lantern pinions were built of wood discs at top and bottom connected by a ring of wooden staves, or rungs which were set into them and served as cogs. The lantern pinions were mounted on the millstone spindles that passed through a wooden bearing, called the "neck" bearing, in the center of the stationary lower bedstone. To provide lubrication for the neck bearing there were usually recesses in the contact surface which were packed with grease-soaked wool or tow.

In the early colonial mills the upper millstone, the runner stone, was attached to the spindle by a "stiff rynd," which engaged the stone by fitting into recesses around the eye. The rynd was usually of cast iron in the form of a straight or curved cross, the arms of which were called "claws." The usual type of rynd was called a four-clawed rynd, but a' few installations had three-clawed rynds. In later mills the eye of the runner stone was fitted with a "balance rynd," "millstone bridge," or "crossbar"; a thick curved iron bar which crossed the eye and fitted into slots sunk about ¾ of an inch into the stone. Frequently two such crosspieces of iron were placed at right angles to each other, with the ends of the balance rynds secured to the stone by lead run into the slots. In the center of the balance rynds was a socket called a "cockeye," the supporting bearing for the runner stone. The pivot point of the millstone spindle, known as the "cock head," fitted into this cockeye. Where the balance rynd was formed of two crosspieces, the ends of one of these pieces would be sunk about 2½ inches deeper into the stone than the ends of the other piece, to allow for the recesses in the stone to accommodate the "driver." This was a heavy piece of cast iron which fitted on the spindle to connect the drive to the stone. Runner stones fitted with balance rynds were much easier to balance than those fitted on stiff rynds, because the stone could swing freely on the cock head and adjust itself to the bedstone. In the case of the stiff rynd, the weight of the runner stone was supported by the ends of the claws at three or four points and was not free to swing. To balance stones pivoted on a cock head, lead was run into crevices in the top of the stone on its lighter side. The millstone spindles were supported by footstep bearings fitted into bridging boxes mounted on bridgetrees that could be raised or lowered. This process, known as "tentering," controlled the clearance between the stones, thus producing finer or coarser meal as required.

Bridging boxes, also known as tram pots, were the housing for the footstep bearing of the millstone spindle. In the early mills these "boxes" were made from strong pieces of hard wood to form tapered sides with a space of about 1½ to 2 inches from the sides of the bearing. In these spaces were inserted wooden wedges to adjust the bearings sideways, thus ensuring that the spindle would run perfectly upright. In later mills the bridging boxes were of cast iron, with wooden wedges used at first in these iron boxes to correct the alignment of the spindle. Later on, there were four set screws, one in each side of the box, adjustment of which could correct the alignment of the spindle. Both methods of adjustment can still be seen in use at the present time.

TENTERING STAFF

Miller Charles Howell is shown testing the texture of the
ground meal. Should a finer or coarser quality be desired,
this can be achieved by varying the distance between the
millstones by use of the tentering staff, visible in the left
foreground, which connects to the bridgetree by the brayer
(not shown in this photo).

To test the millstone spindle for true running, a flat piece of wood called a "jack stick," "tram stick," or "quill stick," having a hole in one end, is placed over the spindle just above the bedstone; in the other end a quill is fixed and adjusted so that it barely scratches the surface of the bedstone. The spindle is turned and if the quill scratches evenly on the level bedstone for the full circle, the spindle is shown to be perfectly upright. If the quill does not scratch evenly all around the stone the footstep bearing is adjusted accordingly.

Some jack sticks are made of thicker timber; from the millstone spindle to a length of about 15 inches, the arm of the jack stick is about 2½ inches thick. At this point the thickness is stepped down to about ¾ of an inch and is continued to the end of the arm, the thinner section being about 9 inches in length on a jack stick used for millstones of 4 to 4½ feet in diameter. At the point where the thickness is stepped down, a saw cut extends into the thicker part of the arm, at the same level as the thinner section, for about 7 inches. Near the end of the thicker section, a wood or iron thumbscrew is inserted. This screw adjusts the thinner section, which has the quill inserted near the end of its radius, so that the quill just touches the surface of the bedstone near its periphery. Some millers dipped the end of the quill into a form of red "paint" usually made from red oxide powder mixed with water, thus marking the stone where the quill touched with a clearly visible mark.

Although there were hundreds of mills scattered throughout the American colonies, they seemed unable to keep up with the increased demand caused by population growth. Faced with this problem, many

QUILL STICK
The Master Miller adjusts the quill stick, used to test the millstone spindle for true running. If the spindle is perfectly upright, the quill should scratch evenly on the level bedstone through a full circle.

entrepreneurs built additional mills, but a more sensible way seemed to be to enlarge the existing ones. Larger and more powerful water wheels were installed, but even more useful was the adoption of gearing systems that permitted more than one pair of stones to be driven from a single water wheel. In a way, this was just another forerunner of the upcoming industrial revolution. Necessity was forcing changes at an amazing rate.

Some water wheel shafts were simply made longer so as to accommodate two face gear wheels, each of which would drive a pair or run of stones; in other installations, the two-step gear train was developed, usually in one of two patterns.

In one system a larger and more strongly constructed face gear was mounted on the water wheel shaft. It had more arms and cants than the face wheels fitted in the earlier mills and was known as the "big" or master face wheel." The big face wheel drove one or two lantern pinions or wallowers on lay-shafts set at right angles. On the wallower shafts were "little face wheels," which meshed into lantern pinions, often called "trundles," on the millstone spindles. The wallower gudgeon nearest the main shaft rested in a sliding block so that either wallower could be disengaged by the use of a lever. This gearing system was referred to as "counter gears."

In the other two-step gearing arrangement, a large face gear was mounted on the water wheel shaft. In this case the gear wheel was usually called the "pit wheel," because the bottom half ran in a pit. The pit wheel meshed into a lantern wallower attached to a

MILL SHAFT WITH TWO FACE WHEELS
In the mill at Philipsburg Manor, the long mill shaft
accommodates two face wheels, each of which engages a
lantern pinion to operate a pair of millstones. The second
lantern pinion is barely visible behind the face wheel in the
upper right corner of this photograph.

COUNTER-GEARING

In the form of two-step gearing known as counter-gearing, the master face wheel (far right) engages a lantern wallower; the wallower shaft turns the little face wheel (here barely visible at far left), which engages another lantern pinion called a trundle (top left), which turns the millstone spindle. Crossing from top left to bottom center in this photo is a lever which could be used to disengage the lantern wallower and thus disconnect the drive to the pair of stones powered from that source.

SPUR GEAR DRIVE
In the form of two-step gearing known as spur gear drive,
the great spur wheel (center) engages lantern pinions
situated around its edge; these in turn are connected to the
millstone spindles. Visible in the foreground is a lever
system which could be used to disengage one of the lantern
pinions, thus disconnecting the drive to the millstones
above it. The mill shown in this photo is located in
Lobachsville, Pennsylvania. Photo: Rex Wailes.

sturdy wooden upright known as the upright shaft. Higher up on the upright shaft, often just above the wallower, was mounted a large spur gear wheel, usually called the "great spur wheel," in which the cogs or teeth were driven into mortices in the edge of the rim, and meshed into lantern or spur pinions attached to the millstone spindles. This arrangement was called "spur gear drive." It usually came from below the millstones and was known as underdrift; but in isolated cases the spur wheel was positioned above the millstones so that the drive came downwards and was known as overdrift. Overdrift was the method most often used in windmills that were equipped with spur-wheel drive. Several pairs of millstones could be arranged around a spur wheel according to its size, though usually there were two, three, or four pairs.

In the overdrift drive, a square or round shaft known as a "quant" brings the drive down from the pinions through the eye of the runner stone and engages on to the top and sides of the rynd or crossbar by a "crotch" or forked end, and sometimes through a "mace" which acts in a similar way to the driver on underdrift drives. The revolving square shaft or squared segment of a round shaft of the quant also acts as a "damsel" (a term we will have occasion to return to). With the overdrift drive it is still necessary to have a spindle below the millstones so that the runner can be balanced and adjusted by tentering.

In most cases provision is made to take the stone pinion or "nut" out of gear. With overdrift drive, the top bearing of the quant is usually housed in a "glut box" which enables half the bearing to be moved to one side and the quant to be taken out of it and swung away from the spur wheel, thus throwing the pinion out of gear.

The stone spindle in underdrift stones cannot be swung aside, because of the fixed position of the bedstone neck bearing. In lantern pinions, some of the staves or rungs were easily removable by tapping out the pegs that held them in working position, so the teeth of the spur wheel did not engage. Some of the cogs in spur pinions were also removable in a similar way. These removable cogs were known as slip cogs.

Some cast iron pinions are mounted on a taper, or on splines or keyways on the spindles. These devices permit the pinions to be raised and held out of gear by a pivoted forked lever, a screw, a rack and pinion, or by two chains which can be wound up on a short shaft.

Although in some instances two-step gearing was developed to permit additional millstones to be driven from a single water wheel, two-step gearing also became necessary when water wheels were built of a larger diameter so that millstones could be operated at a more efficient speed. The speed of the shaft of the water wheel of larger diameter was, of course, slower than that of a smaller water wheel. Because it was not practicable to build up the required speed by one-step gearing, the two-step gearing system was adopted.

Many kinds of hard wood were used in making mill cogs, maple, hickory, white oak, apple, birch, and hornbeam being among the most popular varieties. Similarly, many different types of stone were used in making millstones. It is with this subject that our next chapter is concerned.

The Stone and the Grain

From the very earliest days of milling it became apparent that the quality of the millstones themselves could play a major role in the quality of meal ground by them. Before the Christian era the Romans went to incredible trouble to haul stones for their mills all the way from the banks of the Rhine River.

The most famous early quarry was at Nieder Menting in the Mayen district of the Rhineland, where the stone was a dark bluish-gray lava with even pores. Stones cut from this quarry were known as "Cullin" stones, a corruption of the word Köln, the German name of the city called Cologne in English. To this day millstones are quarried in the district around Mayen and Nieder Menting.

In Roman times the stones were loaded on rafts at Andernach and moved through inland waterways and rivers to the Mediterranean, where they were shipped by sea to Rome. It was much easier for the Dutch, centuries later, to get their Cullin stones by barge down the Rhine. With the Hollanders' merchant fleet serving most of the then-known world, the stones naturally followed Dutch trade and culture to many areas. As with so many other products, names often

67

CULLIN STONE

Millstones of bluish-gray lava quarried in Germany are commonly called Cullin stones. This photo illustrates the use of an old Cullin stone, no longer serviceable for milling, as a stepping stone at the end of a walkway at Philipsburg Manor, Upper Mills. Old, unusable millstones were often put to practical use in this manner.

change to honor the middle man, so these German stones were often called Holland stones. Less frequently they were known as Blue stones, Rhine stones, and Cologne stones.

English settlers in the New World naturally favored stones from the motherland with which they were familiar. Their stones were cut from quarries in the Peak District of southwest Yorkshire and the northeastern perimeter of Derbyshire. The rock in these quarries soon came to be known as Millstone Grit and British millers referred to them as "Peak" or "Grey" stones.

The first ships carrying pioneers to American shores must have borne considerable numbers of millstones from both Germany and England, according to whether the settlers were Dutch or English. The cost of transporting such heavy items across the seas must have been nearly prohibitive, so even before the Indians were subdued venturesome men went exploring for stone that could serve the many mills springing up along the streams of New England, New York, Pennsylvania, Virginia, and the Carolinas. Within a few score years several sources were found.

New York millers found stones near High Falls in Ulster County at a place called The Traps; the material was Shawangunk Conglomerate Grit and the stones were called Esopus Stones. The Esopus Millstone Company, which was a successor to the Bell Millstone Company, had its headquarters at No. 8 Wall Street in Kingston, New York. In advertisements in the milling

PEAK STONE

Millstones quarried in the Peak District of southwest
Yorkshire and northeastern Derbyshire were known as
Peak or Grey stones. This advertisement for Derbyshire
Peak Millstones is from the March 2, 1903, issue of *The
Miller*. The photograph below shows a newly-dressed peak
millstone in the Cranbrook mill in England. Photo: Rex
Wailes.

trade journals around 1875 they described their operations in this way:

> Manufacturers of the well-known Esopus
> Millstones. Runners, Beds, Rollers and Chas-
> ers, Blocks for Glaze Pans, Paving and Color
> Mills and other kinds used by Millers, Mill
> Manufacturers, Paint and Chemical Mills, Pot-
> teries and China Works.

About equally far back from the Hudson, on the
opposite eastern side, quartz-shot sandstone was quarried at Mount Tom in Connecticut. Others stones
came from quarries at Westerly, Rhode Island; in New
Hampshire; in Lancaster, Berkshire, and Carbon
Counties in Pennsylvania; and in Rowan County,
North Carolina.

As the years went by and settlements spread
across the land, millers usually could find usable stone
near at hand to meet their needs. But this was not good
enough for many of the best millers. They knew about
the existence of a French stone that was superior to all
others, and by the middle of the eighteenth century
millstones built up of blocks and sections of French
burr stones were being imported into the American
colonies. At first these stones were assembled in England, but soon the colonists began assembling their
own.

The French burr stone is the best and most popular stone ever discovered for grinding wheat into white
flour. It is a freshwater quartz quarried principally at
La Ferté -sous-Jouarre near the town of Châlons in the

ESOPUS STONE

Conglomerate millstones quarried in New York State
became known as Esopus stones, named for the Esopus
Millstone Company of Kingston, New York, which sold
them. This Esopus stone was uncovered in archaeological
excavations at Philipsburg Manor, Upper Mills, and is
displayed there.

Marne valley in Northern France. This stone is found only in small pieces ranging from about 12 to 18 inches long, 6 to 10 inches wide, by 5 to 10 inches thick, usually embedded in layers of clay. Very infrequently a piece of stone would be quarried large enough to make a millstone in one piece: but usually a French millstone of popular size—4 feet to 4 feet 6 inches—had to be built from separate pieces, or "burrs," as they were usually termed. French burr (or buhr) stones produced a whiter flour from wheat because the extremely hard surface of the stone was far less abrasive than any other stone used. Abrasive stone tended to shred the outer part of the grain of wheat, the bran, into powder. This fine powder bran sifted through the bolting cloth of the flour-dressing machinery or bolters, together with the white part of the wheat meal; and the flour thus produced was of a darker color. By the 1750s French burr stones had become great favorites of colonial millers, particularly those engaged in the export business. The use of French stones enabled them to produce flour of quality comparable to that of the European mills.

Another reason for the superiority of French stones was their high porosity. Some pieces were simply a mass of porous cells; as the stones wore away, new cutting edges appeared. The fact that they could be worked for a long time without being refaced or redressed accounted for their wide popularity with the millers. Some remained in normal use a century or more, but these, of course, were periodically dressed throughout their working life.

The process of building the complete millstones from the blocks of rough French stone began with

FRENCH BURR STONE
French burr millstones were usually composed of a number
of separate pieces of freshwater quartz, each piece called a
"burr," fitted together to form a complete millstone. Visible
in the foreground of this photo is a French burr stone in
which the individual burrs may be seen. Photo: Erich
Hartmann/Magnum.

selecting pieces, usually to form two concentric rings looking rather like keystones of an arch. The number of sectional pieces used varied, depending on the size of the blocks; some French millstones had more than twenty sections, trimmed and dressed to fit and form a perfectly round solid millstone. As in the case of most millstones, the runner had a round hole in the center, usually about 10 inches in diameter, to form the eye, through which the grain was fed. The bedstone was built with a square hole in the center about 10 inches across to accommodate the neck bearing of the driving or balancing spindle. The pieces of stone were cemented or plastered together and bound with iron bands to prevent bursting when the millstones were in use. These bands were usually shrunk on, that is, the iron bands were heated red-hot to make them expand. In this red-hot condition the bands were driven over the edge of the stones; as the bands cooled, they contracted and became extremely tight. The top of the French runner stone was usually finished off with a layer of plaster of Paris to form a slightly convex top. When new, a French runner stone of 4 feet to 4 feet 6 inches in diameter was usually about 12 to 15 inches thick at the circumference, known as the "skirt" of the millstone, and 15 to 18 inches thick at the eye or center and weighed more than 2400 pounds.

The under side of the French bed stone was smoothed off to a perfectly even finish with a layer of plaster of Paris, so that the stone would lie flat on its base. To correct uneven spots, all bedstones, of whatever type of stone, were leveled by driving wooden wedges under the stone in the appropriate spots.

In late-nineteenth-century mills, bed stones were often set in cast-iron "pans," in the base of which, usually at four opposite points, were set-pins, adjustable to correct the level of the stones.

The lower surface of the runner stones and the upper surface of the bed stones were grooved, or "furrowed," in a pattern which caused the meal to flow away from the centers of the stones to their circumferences. The layout of furrows was referred to as the "dress," which generally followed one of two patterns—the "sickle" dress or the "quarter" dress.

Many millstones used in early colonial mills were dressed with the "sickle" or circular furrow dress. This arrangement of furrows was usually marked out on the stones by using the same radius as in the size of the stones; for example, a 4-foot stone had a 2-foot radius. To mark out a left-hand pair of stones, that is, a pair of stones in which the runner revolved counterclockwise, the base point of the compass would be set in the periphery of the stone to the left of the stone eye, with the marker point away from the person using the compass, and conversely for a right-hand millstone. There was a great variation in the number of furrows used, some stones having more than one hundred, while there were others with as few as four. The sickle furrows were usually narrow at the eye and broadened out as they reached the skirt. This spread was as much as from ½ inch at the eye to 2 inches at the skirt, or on larger stones perhaps even more.

The word "quarter" when applied to millstones does not mean a one-fourth part of the area of the stone, but each of the number of sections containing

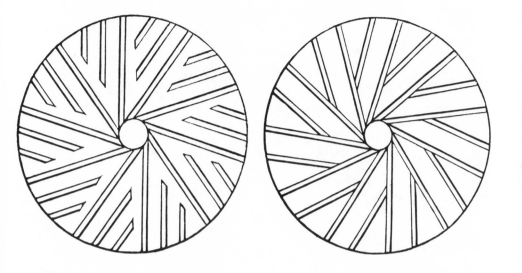

MILLSTONE DRESS

These illustrations depict the main types of millstone dress: "quarter" dress (above), and circular furrow or "sickle" dress (below). The drawings are from *The American Miller and Millwrights' Assistant,* by William Carter Hughes (Detroit, 1850).

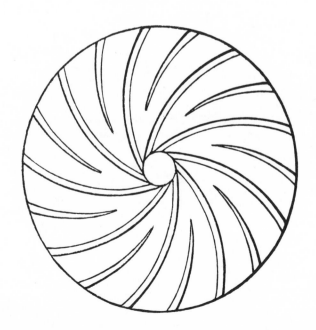

SICKLE DRESS AND QUARTER DRESS

This segment of an old Cullin stone (above) provides a good
example of a millstone in circular furrow or sickle dress.
Below, a French burr millstone in quarter dress at
Philipsburg Manor, Upper Mills. Photo: Erich
Hartmann/Magnum.

the furrows. The quarters were determined by the master furrows. The leading edge of these furrows did not radiate from the dead center of the eye to the skirt but ran tangentially to an imaginary circle around the center of the eye. In a stone which revolved counterclockwise, they were tangential to the left-hand of the center of the eye; and if the stones revolved clockwise, to the right-hand of the center of the eye. The circle was called a draft circle, and its radius was known as the draft; for example, stones with a 6-inch draft circle would have a 3-inch draft. The larger the draft, the more quickly was the ground material carried to the skirt of the stone. Usually there was a smaller draft on stones used mainly for grinding wheat flour, larger drafts being found on stones intended for coarser grinding, as in the case of meal for animal feeds.

Running parallel to the master furrows were secondary furrows. In some cases these would be cut so as to join with the next master furrow, while on other millstones they would terminate just short of the adjoining master furrow. There were many combinations to form the quarters: a millstone might be marked out with twenty quarters of two furrows, nine quarters of six, sixteen quarters of three. In fact, these combinations were as numerous and varied as the individual ideas of millwrights or millers. A popular dress was nine quarters of four furrows, termed by millers: first, the "master furrow"; second, the "journeyman furrow"; third, the "prentice"; and the fourth and shortest, the "butterfly furrow." A millstone dressed with combinations of three furrows had no "fly furrow," and any combinations of two furrows had master and journeyman only. In different areas, of course, different terms might be used for the shorter furrows.

Regardless of the type of dress, the leading edges of the furrows were usually vertical and from ¼ to ¾ of an inch in depth, this depth gradually tapering off to come up to the grinding surface of the stone. The width of furrows in a millstone with quarter dress was usually between 1 and 1¼ inches. The grinding edge at the top of the tapering furrow was known to millers as the "feather edge," and millstones ground feather edge to feather edge.

The furrows were laid out in exactly the same way on both stones, so that, when the runner was turned over for dressing, the design on the grinding faces of both stones was identical. When a pair of millstones were in working position, with the two grinding faces together, as the runner stone revolved the furrows crossed each other to create a positive shearing action, rather like many pairs of scissors in action.

The areas between the furrows, usually about 10 inches wide at the circumference of the stones, were known as "lands," and were dressed with fine lines called "cracks." In a French stone used solely for grinding wheat flour, it was the practice of experienced stonemen to insert about sixteen cracks to the inch, depending on the texture of the stone. In millstones used for grinding corn or animal feed, the cracks varied from three to six per inch, again depending on the ideas of individual millers. The area around the eye of the stones was "faced" off so that when the lands were almost in contact, the stones at this point would be slightly farther apart. This relief permitted the grain to enter between the stones around the eye for preliminary breaking, prior to being ground finer at the skirt of the stones.

To turn the runner stone over for dressing, there was a heavy wooden crane equipped with a large pair of iron tongs, or "bails," the ends of which fitted into holes drilled on opposite sides of the stone to receive them. Sometimes the ends of the tongs were holed so that loose pins could be secured into the bail holes and thence into the corresponding holes in the stone. The bails were fitted with a screwjack, which in the early days was often of hardwood and later of wrought iron. The bails were wide enough to permit the stone to be turned over before being lowered on its back, so that the grinding face could be dressed. The cranes could be swung to one side when not in use. Sometimes the "runner" was turned over by pulley blocks or other devices.

The tools used for dressing or sharpening the grinding faces of the millstones were "mill bills," "mill picks," or "mill pecks." The mill bills were usually shaped like a double-ended wedge and made from cast steel which had been tempered so the chisellike edges would cut the stone. Mill bills were about 7 to 9 inches long and had a hole in the thick center part, into which wooden handles were fitted so the bills could be used somewhat like a hammer.

Sometimes the mill bills were fitted into a "bill thrift," which is a turned wooden handle about 12 to 15 inches in length and shaped almost like a mason's

maul. The head was about 3 inches in diameter, with a
mortice cut to accommodate the bill. The mill "picks"
or "pecks" were sometimes so named to distinguish
them from the chisel-ended bills, because some of
these tools were pointed at the ends in order to "peck"
holes in the surface of the stones; but they were used in
exactly the same way as the bills. When using these
millstone dressing tools, the dresser would usually
half-recline over a cushion or "bist" made of part of a
sack of meal or bran. The bist also steadied his hands
so that the lines or cracks could be cut reasonably
straight in the stone. Stone dressing was a tedious job:
it took a good workman about fourteen hours to dress
each stone.

In later years several types of facing hammers
were used to face off the area around the eye of the
stones. Some were like large chisels with several points
on the cutting edge. Others were a series of several
blades set together almost in the form of a suspension
spring on a road vehicle.

Millers argued about the relative efficiency of the
various dresses used on the stones and the quantity of
grain which could be ground between dressings. However, these measures depended on the fineness of the
grind; because the finer the meal, the more often the
stones needed dressing. It seems, however, that an
average of about fifty tons could be ground on a pair of
stones before redressing was required.

There was always disagreement among millers on
the pattern for dressing a stone, but never any on one
aspect of the operation: it was a mean, backbreaking
chore. Oliver Evans, one of the most famous of early

DRESSING TOOLS

In this photo, a runner stone has been raised and inverted using the iron tongs or bails which are shown gripping the outer edges of the stone. Displayed on the surface of the stone are various types of dressing tools, including a facing hammer (far left), assorted mill bills (center), and a bill thrift (far right). Visible in the background is the quill stick used to test the spindle for true running.

MILLER DRESSING A MILLSTONE

Miller Charles Howell uses a mill bill set in a bill thrift to dress a runner stone which has been inverted using the iron tongs or bails suspended from the stone crane. As he works, the miller reclines upon a cushion or "bist" made of a partially-filled sack of meal or bran; this helps to steady his arm as he dresses or sharpens the stone.

writers on milling in this country, insisted that the cutting edges of the grooves be sharp. A dull stone, he wrote, "kills or destroys that lively quality of the grain, that causes it to ferment and raise in baking; it also makes the meal so clammy it sticks to the cloth and chokes up the meshes in bolting [sifting]."

Pity the poor miller who dressed his own stones. For thirteen or fourteen hours, with very little time taken off to eat or rest, he chipped away at the furrows with his chisels, bills, and thrift. In England this work was often done by itinerant workers, but in America the miller usually dressed his own stones.

So eager were English millers to have this onerous labor performed by someone else, careless workers often tried to pose as good stone dressers. The cautious miller, however, insisted that the jobseeker "show his metal" before hiring him. So the man bared his left hand and forearm. If there were many small bluish spots showing where minute particles of steel from the chisel had imbedded themselves in the flesh, the miller knew he had a good worker.

To test the grinding surfaces of millstones a wooden paint staff is used, much like a "straight edge," and usually about 4 feet in length, 5 inches in depth and about 4 inches in width. The testing edge has marking "paint" brushed on with a paint brush. The paint is often made of "raddle" or "tiver," a composition of red oxide powder mixed with water. Other "paints" were made from red clay, scalded soot, and, in later years, domestic washing blue was often utilized. Before using the staff any surplus paint is removed by a dry paint brush. The painted staff is rotated around the grinding surfaces on the stones, which may need to be dressed or "flawed" down. The lands of the stones, the areas between the furrows about 10 inches in from the circumference, should carry the staff and be marked evenly all over. After this operation, the staff is repainted, before being used on the next stone.

In the old days staffs were made of a solid piece of hardwood, often oak, walnut, or mahogany. These solid staffs were subject to warping, however, so later on paint staffs were made of laminated wood, soft or hard. A selected piece of wood, usually about the same size as the solid staff, was cut lengthwise into three or four strips, and alternate pieces reversed in position. The strips were then glued together and further secured by brass screws. This later type of staff is, of course, much less inclined to warp with changing climatic conditions.

The accuracy of the paint staff is tested, or "proved," by a proof staff. This is a machined cast-iron plate about 4 feet long and about 4 ½ inches wide, usually mounted on the wall of the mill in a wooden case with a hinged lid. A small amount of machine oil is smeared on the proof staff, and the paint staff is then lightly rubbed along the surface. The high spots of the wooden staff are thereby marked by the oil and these high spots are then scraped off by a steel scraper, or more often, by a piece of glass. Sometimes a short staff about 2 feet in length, known as the eye staff, is used to test the face of the millstone around the center or eye division.

An English miller who sent directions for tempering mill bills to the magazine *Milling* many years ago recommends that the tools to be resharpened be

PAINT STAFF AND PROOF STAFF

In the photograph above, Miller Charles Howell is shown using a paint staff, or "stone staff," to determine if the face of the stone is level. The illustration below depicts various tools used in stone dressing, including in the foreground a metal proof staff, or "prover," used to test the accuracy of the paint staff. Illustration courtesy of Rex Wailes.

The above engraving shows the Stone Dresser engaged in renewing the "Dress" or grinding surface of the Millstone. The various tools, &c., are as follows:—

Fig. 1. The Mill Bills.
" 2. Handles for the same
" 3. The Stone Staff, for ascertaining if the surface of the Stone is true.
" 4. Case for the Stone Staff.
" 5. Burr for rubbing the face of the Stone.

Fig. 6. Colouring matter for the Stone Staff.
" 7. Dusting Brush.
" 8. Furrows or channels in the Stone.
" 9. Grinding surfaces or "land" of the Stone
" 10. Stone Eye.
" 11. Metal Prover, in wood case, for testing the accuracy of the Stone Staff.

"drawn out" by a blacksmith to the required thinness. The fire in the forge is not large but is maintained carefully. In a closed workshop—so the color can better be judged—the edge of the bill is heated to a blood or cherry red about ¾ of an inch up.

With the bill held perfectly straight down, it should be dipped into the cooling liquor, just to cover the red part for eight seconds or so, longer if the bills are thick, shorter if very thin. If the bill is brittle it has been dipped too long; if too soft, it needs a longer dip.

The English miller also says the color induced by the fire and dipping should be "as blue as a raven's feather." The bill should be cooled slowly, near the fire, so no cool draft strikes it. When tempering more than one bill, they should not be allowed to touch one another while cooling, as this will cause heat to be transferred in unequal amounts, damaging the tempering.

It takes about an hour for the bills to cool before the other ends should be tempered. The cooling liquor should be stirred with a clean stick several times, as otherwise the mixture cools unevenly.

> This expert's recipe for the cooling mixture is:
>   2 gallons of rainwater
>   ½ ounce of unkilled spirits of salts
>   1 ounce of blue vitriol powder
>   2 ounces niter powder.

If the bills are tempered in frosty weather, the miller suggests inserting a red-hot poker into the liquor before dipping the first bill, to warm it.

Stone case, tun, vat, hoop, and husk were the names applied to the wooden casings around the millstones, which were often made from a soft wood such as white pine or poplar. The casings were made 2 to 4 inches wider than the diameter of the millstones. Some runner stones were fitted with a tag known as a "sweeper"; as the stone revolved, this tag would sweep between the edge of the stones and the case and thus carry the meal to the spout opening. In many instances, however, the meal was carried to the spout by the movement of the revolving stone.

On top of the stone case stood the "horse" or "hopper ladder," made of wood and usually with four legs that fitted into slots in the case. The horse held the hopper in position; and at the base of the hopper was fitted a slide which controlled the amount of grain that was fed into the "shoe." A reciprocating movement was conveyed to the shoe by a "damsel." This was usually a short shaft of wood attached to the top of the center of the rynd in the eye of the runner stone so that, as the stone turned, the damsel revolved with it. The corners of the damsel tapped against a block or "rap" on the inside of the shoe, causing it to vibrate and feed an even trickle of grain into the eye of the stone.

This clever contrivance was a very noisy piece of equipment in the mill, chattering ceaselessly from the moment the work began until the water wheel was disengaged and stopped turning. Some unsung, unhonored miller with a sense of humor dubbed this device the "damsel"—and in light of the sexism prevalent at the time no one ever had to spell out the reason why. In later mills the damsels were frequently made

STONE CASE, HORSE, AND HOPPER
The Master Miller checks the quality of the ground meal
emerging from the spout opening in the "stone case," the
circular wooden frame surrounding the working pair of
millstones. Atop the stone case is the "horse" or "hopper
ladder," a four-legged wooden frame which holds in
position the "hopper," which feeds the grain into the
"shoe," a tapering wooden trough through which the grain
is fed to the stones. Photo: Gene Maggio/NYT Pictures.

of iron, but they were as noisy as the wooden ones.

After the grain had passed between the stones, it dropped down a spout to a lower floor or level, usually discharging into a wooden trough for cooling purposes. From here it was scooped or shoveled into barrels or sacks.

In the first of the small mills grain was tipped directly into the millstone hoppers from sacks or barrels but later, larger mills had bins or garners, as they were called, on the upper floor. Grain fed from the bins down through a spout to the hoppers. The second floor of such mills also provided a place to dry damp grain and to store supplies for later use.

The Search For Quality

Colonial mills advanced in efficiency as the decades rolled by. While at first the water wheels provided power only for the stones, later they were used to power sack hoists to lift grain from wagons to the upper floors of mills, and for other purposes.

Some of these sack hoists were operated by a lantern pinion which engaged the cogs of a face gear at horizontal right angles. The lantern pinion was attached to a windlass barrel which turned continuously as the mill was in operation. There was a rope with slack turns around the barrel; the other end of the rope would be over a pulley, usually in a beam which projected from the gable end of the roof just above a doorway, so that the end of the rope with a hook on it would be outside the end of the building. To lift barrels or sacks into the top floor of the mill from carts, or perhaps boats, the hook would be attached to the barrel or sack. Then the person outside would signal to the men inside the mill to tighten the rope around the revolving windlass barrel. Thus the rope would be pulled upward outside and lift its load to the top of the mill. Sack hoists eventually became quite elaborate, with wooden friction clutches, or slack leather belt

HOISTING GRAIN INTO THE BINS

Storage areas for grain, known as bins or garners, were often located on the upper floor of a mill. Sack hoists were used to lift bags of grain up to the bins for storage.

mechanisms, which permitted engaging or disengaging by control ropes from the point where the sacks were taken into the mill.

Numerous accounts of Anglo-Saxon times tell of the difference between the flour used to make bread for the masters of households and that for bread for the servants. The former was sifted carefully by hand until the chaff and bran were removed, leaving a fine white flour, while the servants had to make do with unsifted flour, not unlike today's graham flour.

As millers took over more of the business from individual households, they learned that sifted flour brought a better price so they undertook to speed up the process. Before the time of Columbus bakers had been left to clean and sift their own flour, but when power became available for the process, the miller took over this profitable step.

First of all, the miller sought to clean the grain before it passed through his millstones. Crude fans that forced air through a chamber blew out chaff and other foreign material. These fans were often powered by the same water wheel that drove the stones, although some were still turned by hand. In the years before metal became all-important, the wooden-framed sieves were cylindrical and the fan-driven blast of air, being contained, did a fairly efficient job.

Much more important was the sifting of the meal after the grain had been ground. Like other equipment, the first devices to achieve this were hand-turned, but the millers soon realized the value of water-driven machinery and invented sifters actuated by a power takeoff from the main shaft of the mill.

BOLTING MACHINE

Ground meal could be sifted and separated into lots according to texture using a bolting machine. The type shown here used an inclined rectangular sieve covered with progressively coarser grades of sifting cloth to separate the grain into finer or coarser grinds.

Some bolting machines were rectangular, inclined sieves, mounted in a frame, one end of which supported a hopper. From this hopper the meal flowed on to the sieve which usually had fine-screen cloth at the top and coarser cloth at the bottom end. The finest flour dropped through the top section, the coarser through the lower part, and the bran and middlings went over the end. The sieve was vibrated by a square shaft of wood on which the upper end of the sieve rested, and which was rotated by a handle.

Another type of bolting machine consisted of cylindrical, square, or polygonal reels, which in the early days were about 6 feet long and possibly 2 feet in diameter. Flour-dressing reels had a central wooden shaft from which short spokes radiated, with wooden slats laid lengthwise on the outer edge of the spokes. These slats had rounded edges and were closer together in the case of a cylindrical reel; in the case of polygonal reels, there would be as many lengthwise slats as there were sides. For example, there would be six lengthwise slats for a hexagonal reel, while there would be only four for a square one.

This light wooden framework was covered with bolting cloth of three different degrees of fineness. The finest was at the head end of the reel and the coarsest at the foot or tail end. The reel was tilted slightly, higher at the head than at the foot. As the reel was slowly revolved, the wheat meal was fed in at the head end. The finest particles went through the fine-meshed cloth at the head section. Through the center section of the reel, covered with a coarser cloth, went some of the material left over from the first section of

REEL-TYPE BOLTING MACHINE
This example of a reel-type bolting machine is in the
Oakdale Grist Mill at Connetquot River State Park on Long
Island. Photo: New York State Parks Commission.

the reel and some larger particles making up the middlings. The product going through the coarsest cloth nearest the foot was called "middlings," "sharps" or "shorts." The remaining rough particles or bran passed out of the reel at its lower end. Square or polygonal reels gave a more positive sifting process because of the tumbling action created by the revolving flat sides. Under the varying meshed sections of the reels were placed wooden dividers to guide the different grades to spouts that filled sacks or barrels positioned below.

After about 1730 most mills of any size drove the flour bolters by water power. Many mills had, under the meal spouts, inclined rectangular sieves that received their reciprocating motion from a connecting rod activated by a simple wooden cam on the head of a lantern pinion or a cam attached to the millstone spindle. These simple types of sieve were often used for cornmeal or buckwheat flour, and covered with cloth woven in meshes of various sizes or wire mesh. Toward the end of the colonial period, the large merchant mills had quite elaborate systems of bolting.

The cylindrical or polygonal reels were much larger, sometimes exceeding 20 feet in length and 30 inches in diameter. Some mills would have several reels enclosed in wooden cabinets, so that the flour would not be blown around the mill. In many of these mills, the middlings were returned to the millstones for further grinding and then fed back on to the reels for additional sifting.

Parallel with the improvements in the sifting machinery went improvements in the material that did the actual sifting. Early written history is replete with mention of man's insistence on finer flour. The Bible tells of Abraham instructing his wife Sarah to use "fine" meal when preparing her hearth bread and the Egyptians commonly used sieves made of woven papyrus or other grasses to gain the same end. Roman millers used woven grass sieves but also employed sections of tanned cowhide which they pierced with tiny holes to get differing grades of meal—the smaller the holes, the finer the meal.

In medieval times a new development came about when German millers began using woolen bags to sift flour. The meal was placed in the bag, which was then shaken or struck repeatedly with a stick. Inevitably this device was eventually automated by changing the bag into a sleevelike container and having the beating done by a paddle worked by a ratchet wheel attached to the spindle of the millstone. The flour fell through the cloth and the tailings worked out at the far end.

Because of the rough treatment given the woolen material, it soon wore out and millers looked around for a stronger fabric. About the time the Pilgrims were struggling to build Plymouth into a permanent, safe home, patents were issued in Great Britain for the making of woven wire cloth. A century later a Scot named John Milne invented a sifting reel that rotated instead of being shaken. It was a true breakthrough.

This reel made possible the use of much finer fabrics and it wasn't long before silken gauze from the East Indies became the favored material. All this changed when Dutch weavers in Haarlem began producing an even stronger cloth. One of the innovators was a refugee Huguenot, Abraham Le Grand, who wove a superior fabric at the end of the seventeenth century. It is intriguing to note that the firm founded in 1728 at his death, De Weduwe, Le Grand and Belain, remained in business until 1902.

Bolting cloth was made with wool, linen, and even horsehair, but it was Swiss weavers, copying techniques originating in the Haarlem mills, who perfected the silk cloth that became the standard until modern times. Silk was very reliable and could easily be woven into cloth with different-sized openings to sift varying grades of flour.

Yet silk, like other early fabrics, had one shortcoming. Moisture absorbed from the air caused it to become taut; lack of moisture caused it to grow too slack. This problem was overcome when American inventors produced the great artificial silk—nylon—using chemicals in coal, water, and the atmosphere. Nylon maintained its tautness with little change and it lasted three times longer than natural silk. Since its invention, sifting cloth has been made almost exclusively from this artifical fiber.

The changes and innovations that came about in Europe were reflected in America, where millers tried to keep pace with the times, even if on occasion a bit behind their brother millers overseas.

Until after the Revolutionary War most mills in America remained relatively small, turning out just enough flour and meal to satisfy the needs of the community. The miller was paid in kind, keeping a percentage of the ground meal for himself. The "miller's toll" ranged from 10 to 20 percent. By selling it to those who had no grain to grind, he was able to convert it into cash for himself and family or, at least, to have

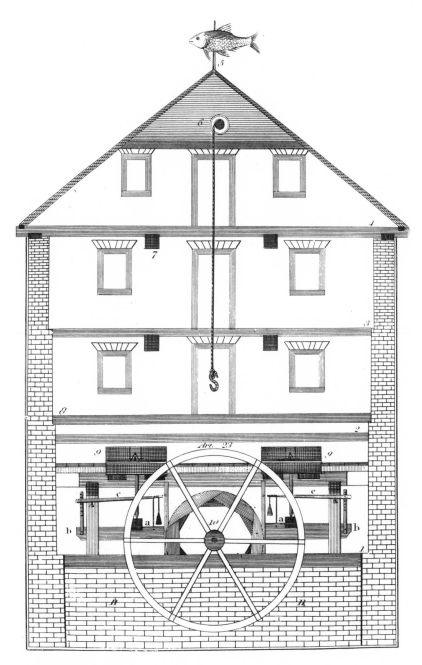

MERCHANT MILL

Some large commercial or merchant mills expanded to several stories and contained multiple pairs of stones. This design for one such mill is by Oliver Evans.

something with which to barter. These small mills, which came to be called "custom mills," had small outputs, averaging about three or four bushels an hour.

Some few mills, especially nearer the large cities, expanded into large stone-housed establishments many stories high with as many as six pairs of millstones powered by a single water wheel. These "merchant mills" packed the flour in barrels and shipped it to markets all over this country as well as abroad. By the late 1700s and early 1800s such mills were a far cry from the rustic wooden mills that had been a hallmark of colonial life.

Of Winds and Tides

Long after the Greeks and Romans mastered the art of harnessing water power to activate their mills, other men turned to the wind, seeking similar surcease from man's labor. History records the mention of a millwright in Persia who was obviously engaged in building a mill to be operated by the winds blowing across the flat deserts of his native land. The year was A.D. 644. Then there is mention of a windmill at Seistan, also in Persia, in A.D. 915. These Persian mills had sails working horizontally, and it seems evident that early artisans had mastered the use of the wind, fickle though it is, by erecting movable sails to tap its energy.

History picks up the thread again when Genghis Khan and his hordes roared out of the Mongolian wastes and subjugated many of the civilized nations around the Persian Gulf. Genghis Khan was not too busy looting and burning to note the windmills in Persia. Visualizing their great potential as a means of irrigating the fields of China, he sent numerous millwrights whom he had taken prisoner back to China to teach farmers there how to use wind to power irrigation systems. For the next seven centuries the Chinese relied heavily on horizontal windmills to keep crops growing in arid areas.

These early windmills derived from the ancient horizontal mills, using no gears. The wind blew in through one opening in the mill building and out of the other, turning the sails on the way. Because these mills were not satisfactory except in areas where the wind blew from one direction only, it was not long before millwrights turned to the Roman watermill with its horizontal axis as a model for better effectiveness. It is thought that the Crusaders brought the idea for these mills to France and England from the Levant, as they are first mentioned in both countries in the twelfth century.

The early versions of the geared windmills were built on solid posts so the sails could be turned to face into the wind, and were known as post mills. This type of windmill appeared in France in 1180, in England in 1191, and in that part of Syria held by the Crusaders in 1190.

The wooden boxlike body of a post mill contains the gearing, millstones, and machinery, and carries the sails. The body of the mill is mounted on an upright post which is in turn supported by a four-legged trestle. An example of a reconstructed eighteenth-century post mill can be seen at Colonial Williamsburg in Virginia.

Early in the fourteenth century the "tower mill" was developed in France. Its gearing and millstones were placed in a fixed tower with a rotating roof, or "cap," which carried the "wind shaft" on which the sails were mounted. The cap could be turned on a track, or "curb," on top of the tower. Towers built of stone or brick were usually round. Timber towers, usually octagonal and tapering, were known in England as

POST MILL

Windmills built on solid posts so that the sails could be
turned to face into the wind were known as post mills. The
example of a post mill shown here is Robertson's Mill at
Colonial Williamsburg, Virginia. Drawing by Robert Fink.

TOWER MILL
The tower windmill shown here, equipped with patent sails and an automatic fantail, is located in Pakenham, West Suffolk, England. Photo: Rex Wailes.

SMOCK MILLS

Two examples of smock windmills: above, at Gardiner's Island, New York, the sole remaining smock mill of five which were once located there (photo: Rex Wailes). On next page, the Barham Smock Windmill, with a fantail, at Kent, England; this mill has been destroyed since this photo was taken.

"smock mills," so called because the tapering sides of the mill gave something of the appearance of a man wearing a smock. Many of the roofs were thatched, heightening the effect.

While mills were perfected originally to grind cereal grains, the Dutch in the early 1400s saw their potential for helping to drain sea water from reclaimed land behind their dikes. Instead of powering millstones, the sails gave their energy to scoop wheels which lifted water from a low to a higher level. These mills were invaluable to the Netherlands for generations.

In order for windmills to run efficiently the sails must face squarely into the prevailing wind. To achieve this the first millers attached a tailpole to the movable body of the post mill and to the cap of tower mills. Men moved the pole to direct the sails into the wind. Here again, arduous manual labor became supplanted when in 1746 Edmund Lee of England invented an automatic device to keep the sails facing correctly. He did it with a "fantail," a small vaned wheel set at right angles to the main sails. Whenever the wind changed direction it turned the vanes of the fantail which was connected to gears on the track at the top of the main portion of the mill. This turned the big sails again into the teeth of the wind.

Windmills were not as efficient as watermills, for the obvious reason that there were many days when the wind did not blow hard enough to turn the sails. But, inefficient though they were, they ran without much attention and served man well where there was no water power, until the steam engine and electric generator came along.

Both the English and Dutch brought windmills to this country, and within four or five decades the lowlands of Cape Cod, Long Island, and southern Rhode Island and Connecticut were dotted with mills. They were most popular on Cape Cod and Long Island, where there were few streams suitable for operating water wheels.

It is nearly impossible for the citizen of the late twentieth century to envision the environs of New York Harbor as it looked in the days of Dutch supremacy there. Yet on both sides of the lower Hudson mouth, along Jamaica Bay and in the hinterland behind Sandy Hook, New Jersey, there were scores of windmills turning in the onshore and offshore breezes which made the vicinity of the coast such a good place for windmills.

The Dutch themselves were amazed at what their colonial brothers had wrought in the New World.

"As we sailed into the harbor," wrote one traveler from the Netherlands, "the horizon was pierced by scores of windmills, taller than any we have seen elsewhere."

Somehow this remark reflected the spirit of the early settlers and those who followed in their tracks: there was something about the new land that encouraged bigger and more daring enterprises among those who dared to leave the Old World for a challenging life in the New.

Today there are more windmills of the old type surviving on eastern Long Island, New York, than in any other part of the United States. The Long Island windmills are all of the smock type. Nearly all are full of interesting machinery, including centrifugal

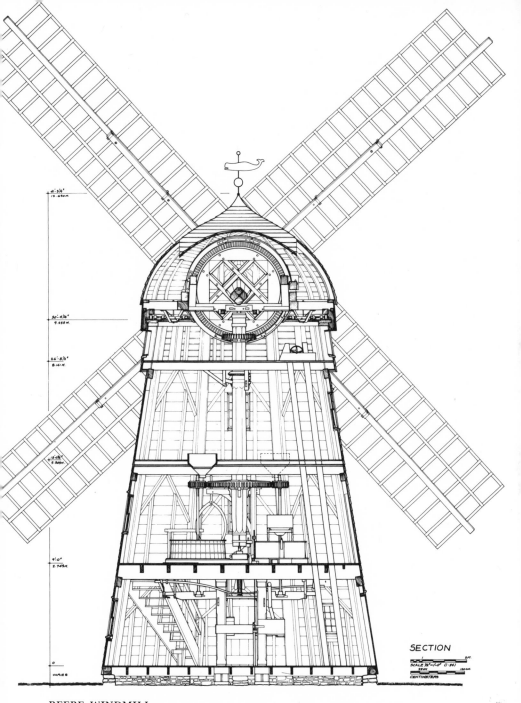

BEEBE WINDMILL

This cutaway drawing of the Beebe Windmill in Suffolk
County on Long Island shows the overdrift, spur-gear drive
mechanism by which power is harnessed to drive two pair of
millstones. Drawing: Historic American Engineering
Record, National Park Service, by Chalmers G. Long,
Jr., 1976.

governors, which maintain the preset gap between the millstones, hence controlling the fineness of grinding. This form of tentering by automatic governors was probably the first successful feedback mechanism. In England in 1787 Thomas Mead was granted a patent for a "Regulator for Wind and Other Mills," which shows centrifugal governors applied to the machinery of windmills.

Old records reveal that the many ferries that connected Staten Island with Manhattan, Brooklyn, the Connecticut littoral and Long Island, and the Massachusetts shore with Nantucket and Martha's Vineyard—all depending on sails in those days—were skippered by masters who could read weather signs wherever they existed. Some of the ferry owners advertised that they would operate "daily services except when the windmills on the opposite shore have taken in their sails."

One reason for the existence of so many windmills on Long Island was the need for salt in the growing towns nearby. Many of the wind-driven mills were used to pump water from the sea into great basins enclosed by dikes. There the water evaporated and the salt was scraped up, much as it is done today on the Spanish coast near Cadiz and Jerez de la Frontera, but not by wind power any more.

As early as 1640, only two decades after the Dutch began putting their roots down at the mouth of the Hudson, there were windmills on Manhattan Island. When Jasper Danckaerts, a Dutchman, came to America in 1679 looking for a place to establish his fellow Labadists in a refuge from religious persecu-

LONG ISLAND WINDMILL
Among the many windmills standing today on Long Island is the smock mill (right) located in the town of Watermill in Suffolk County. Drawing: Historic American Engineering Record, National Park Service, by Kathleen Hoeft, 1976.

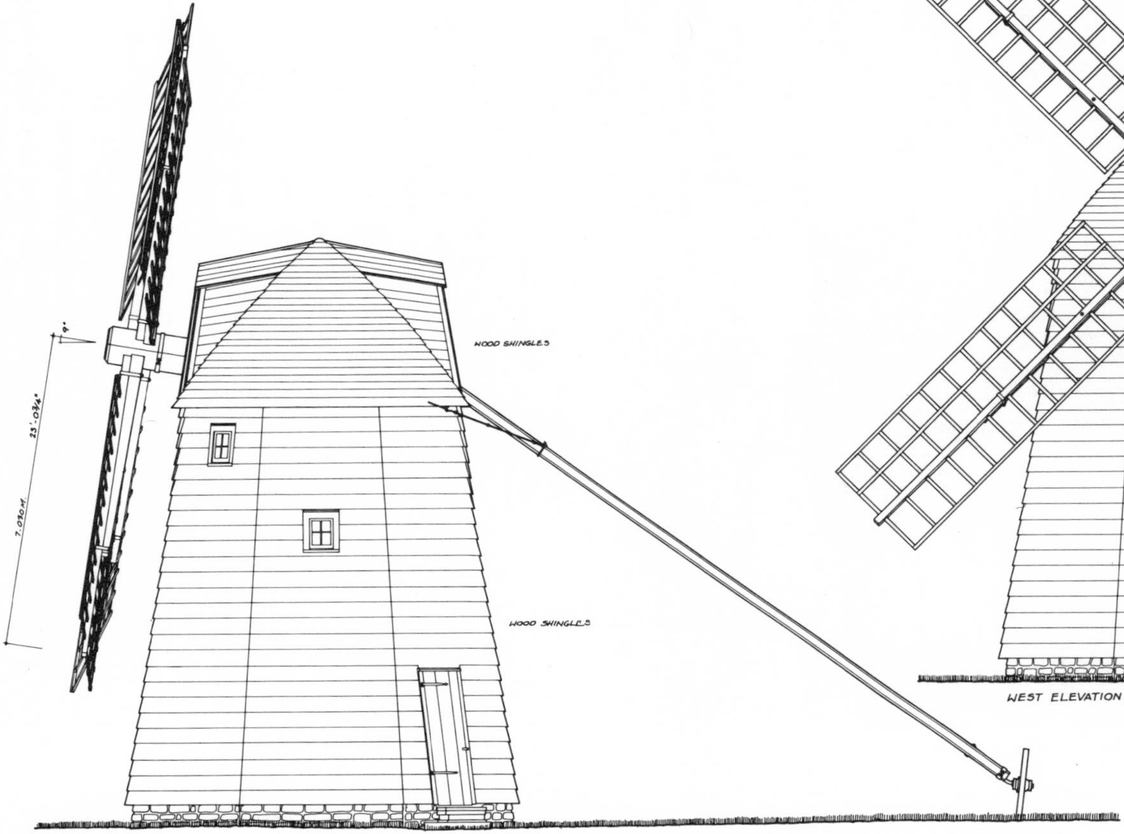
9°
7.030 M.
23'-0 3/4"
WOOD SHINGLES
WOOD SHINGLES
SOUTH ELEVATION

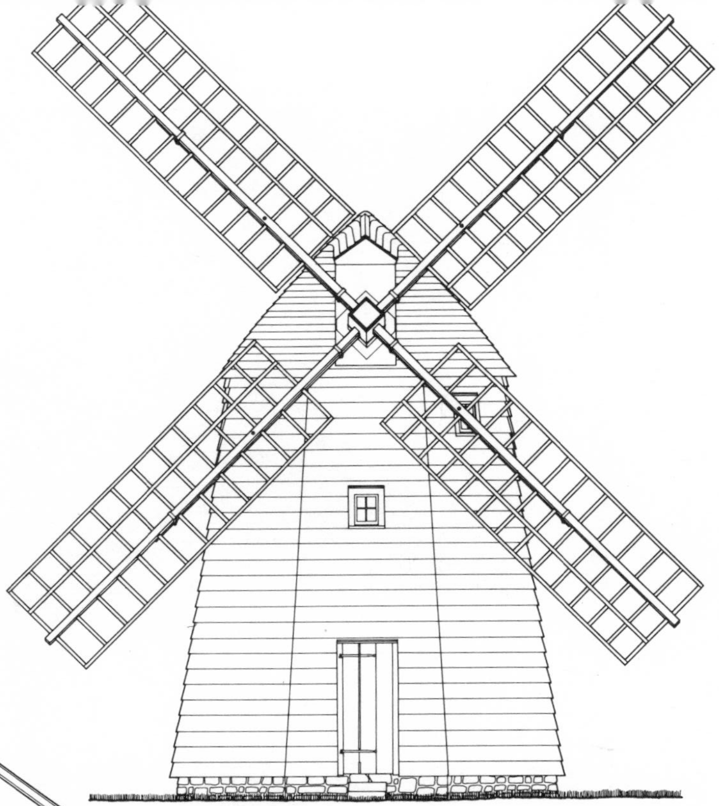
WEST ELEVATION

ELEVATIONS

SCALE 3/8" = 1'-0" (1:32)

1 5 10 FT.

METERS

CENTRIFUGAL GOVERNOR

Centrifugal governors (above) are used in windmills to maintain a preset distance between the stones. The centrifugal governor mechanism shown here is in the windmill at Watermill, Long Island. Photo: Rex Wailes.

HOOK WINDMILL

The drawings which follow on the next three pages show the exterior of the Hook Windmill, located in Suffolk County, Long Island, and interior details of its structure and machinery. Drawings: Historical American Engineering Record, National Park Service, by Kathleen Hoeft, 1975.

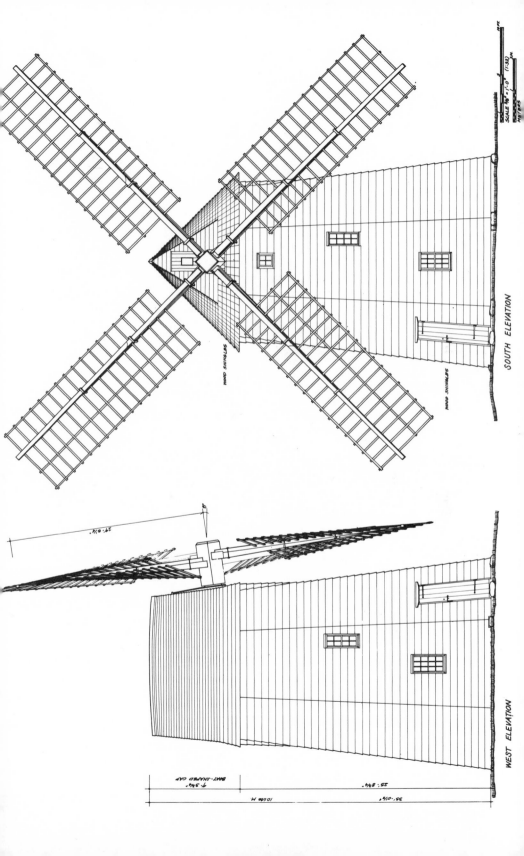

WOOD SHINGLES

WOOD SHINGLES

SOUTH ELEVATION

WEST ELEVATION

SCALE ⅜" = 1'-0" (1:32)

METERS

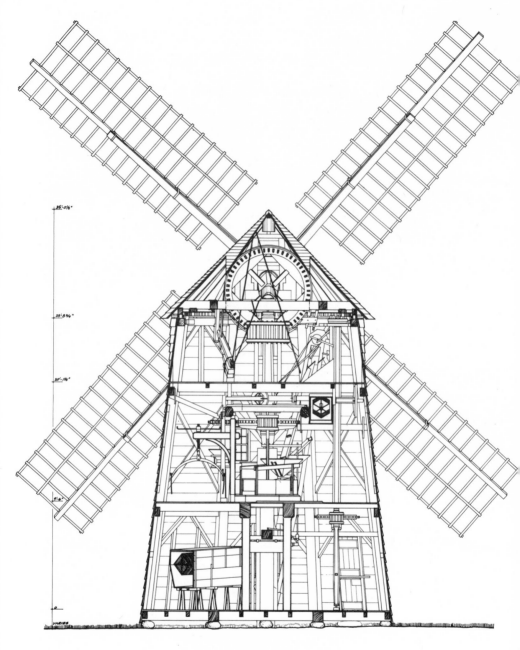

SECTION A-A

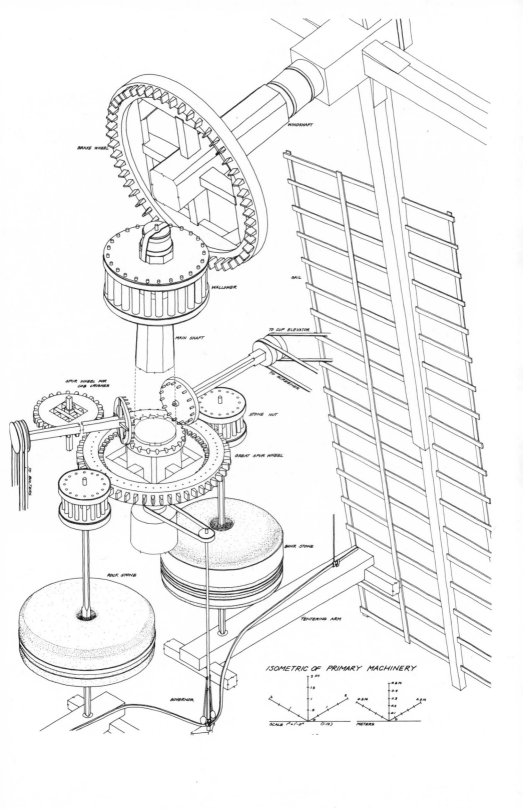

WINDSHAFT

BRAKE WHEEL

WALLOWER

SAIL

MAIN SHAFT

TO CUP ELEVATOR

TO SCREENER

SPUR WHEEL FOR
COB CRUSHER

STONE NUT

TO BOLTERS

GREAT SPUR WHEEL

ROCK STONE

BUHR STONE

TENTERING ARM

GOVERNOR

ISOMETRIC OF PRIMARY MACHINERY

SCALE 1"=1'-0"   (1:12)   METERS

HOOK WINDMILL GEARING
A complex system of gearing in the Hook Windmill is used to drive two pair of millstones as well as other devices such as bolting machinery. The photograph above shows the great spur wheel and one of the two stone nuts in the Hook Windmill.

tion, he wrote of his visit in a journal which was later published as *Journal of a Voyage to New York*. Besides writing the text, he also drew sketches of the colony. There is one showing lower Manhattan with several windmills clearly evident, one of them where City Hall Park is now. By then there were also several watermills on the island, fed by streams long since lost in the march of urbanization. Interestingly enough, the coat of arms of New York City has a set of windmill sails in its design.

Both water-driven mills and those powered by wind had their advantages and disadvantages. The former were useless in those areas where the streams froze in winter. Records indicate that the winters of the eighteenth century were particularly severe and many a miller saw his water wheel torn away or damaged by ice. On the other hand, the windmills were useless on calm days, which came most often in the summer—so, in a way, the two types of mills complemented each other.

There was one other type of mill which antedated steam by several centuries—the tidemill. It was a close relative of the water-driven mills built beside streams and powered by water held behind dams. The main difference was that instead of relying on water coming downstream and filling a pond, the tidemill used the energy from the tidal water that flooded into basins or river valleys at high tide.

Dams were constructed to hold the water back at its highest level. In most cases a hinged sluice gate in the dam would be forced open by the incoming tide, and thus the pond or valley would be filled. As the tide

began to ebb and the water started to flow outward, the
sluice gate would close and the water behind it would
be trapped at the high level. When the tide had gone
out sufficiently, there was a head of water available to
power a water wheel. The operation of such mills was
confined to two periods in the twenty-four-hour day,
each of about five and a half hours, and of course these
periods came at varying times within the twenty-four
hours. Because of the relatively small difference in the
height of the water at high and low tides, tidal mills
virtually all used undershot wheels.

SEAL OF THE CITY OF NEW YORK
Symbols on the Seal of the City of New York reflect
elements of its early commerce, including beavers symbolic
of the early fur trade, and a set of windmill sails, a common
site along the shores of Manhattan Island during the
colonial period. Courtesy of Museum of the City of
New York.

The thrifty Dutch settlers were not long in recognizing the potential of the powerful tides running into the creeks of New Amsterdam, now New York, so as early as 1635 a man named Gerritson was operating a tidemill in what is now known as Flatbush, then called Midwout. In fact, this mill survived well into the twentieth century. Today a working example of a tidemill can be seen at the Saddle Rock Grist Mill, Great Neck, New York, a town on the north shore of Long Island.

Inventors to this day are still toying with the idea that tidal power can be harnessed to generate large amounts of electricity. Much money has been spent on studies of such projects, the most dramatic being at Passamaquoddy Bay in Maine, several points in the Bay of Fundy between New Brunswick and Nova Scotia, and the River Severn in England.

The first windmill erected in America was built for Governor Yeardley in Virginia in 1621. Ten years later there was another windmill at Watertown, Massachusetts. The first watermill was put up at Dorchester in 1633 and another two years later at Ipswich, both

VAN WYCK-LEFFERTS TIDEMILL
The drawings on the following three pages show the exterior and interior details of the Van Wyck-Lefferts Tidemill, located at Mill Cove Pond, Lloyd Harbor, in Suffolk County, Long Island. Water which flowed in at high tide was dammed up behind the sluice gate, then released at low tide to drive the water wheel which powered two pair of millstones. Drawings: Historic American Engineering Record, National Park Service, by Lawrence Nicoletti and Kathleen Hoeft, 1975.

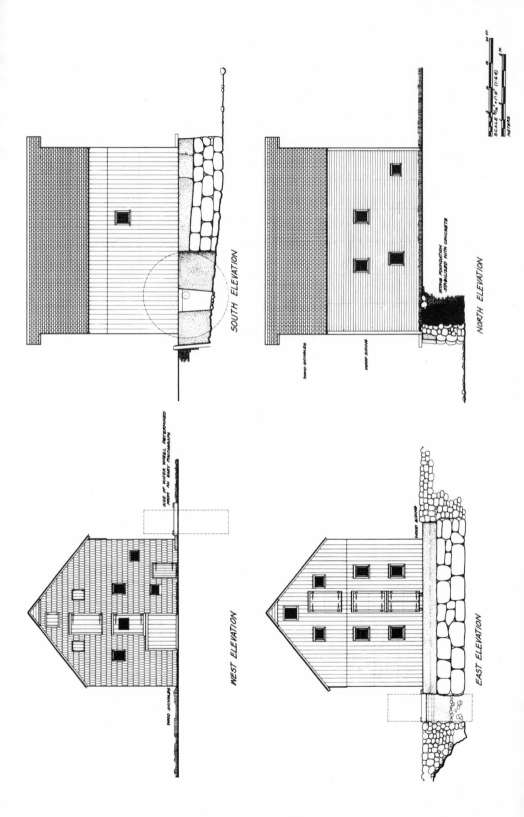

SOUTH ELEVATION

NORTH ELEVATION

WEST ELEVATION

EAST ELEVATION

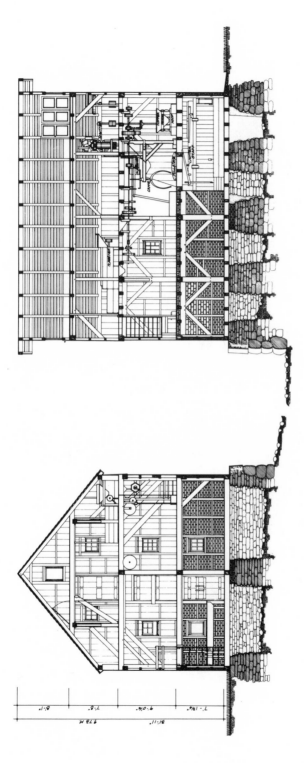

SECTION A-A

SECTION B-B

SCALE 1/4" = 1'-0" (1:48)
METERS

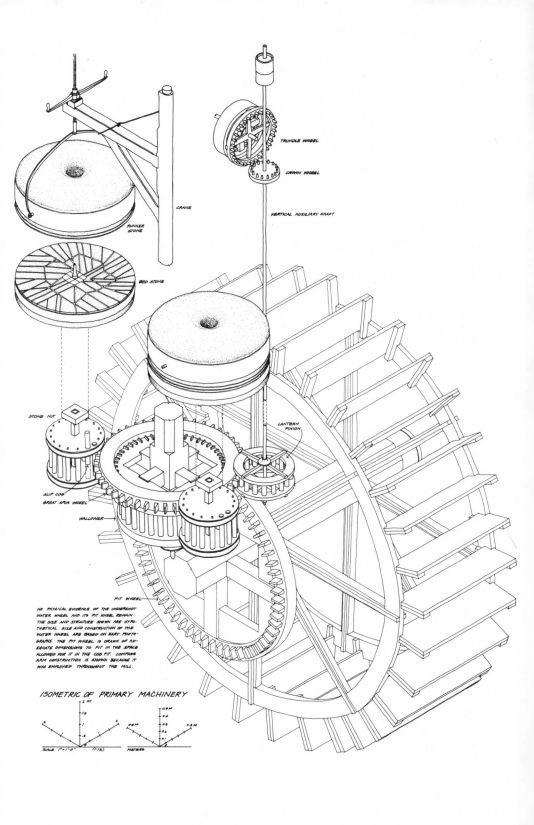

CRANE

RUNNER
STONE

BED STONE

TRUNDLE WHEEL

CROWN WHEEL

VERTICAL AUXILIARY SHAFT

STONE NUT

LANTERN
PINION

SLIP COG
GREAT SPUR WHEEL

WALLOWER

PIT WHEEL

NO PHYSICAL EVIDENCE OF THE UNDERSHOT
WATER WHEEL AND ITS PIT WHEEL REMAIN:
THE SIZE AND STRUCTURE SHOWN ARE HYPO-
THETICAL. SIZE AND CONSTRUCTION OF THE
WATER WHEEL ARE BASED ON EARLY PHOTO-
GRAPHS. THE PIT WHEEL IS DRAWN OF AD-
EQUATE DIMENSIONS TO FIT IN THE SPACE
ALLOWED FOR IT IN THE COG PIT. COMPASS
ARM CONSTRUCTION IS SHOWN BECAUSE IT
WAS EMPLOYED THROUGHOUT THE MILL.

ISOMETRIC OF PRIMARY MACHINERY

1 FT.
.5

SCALE 1"=1'-0"   (1/12)

0.8M.
0.7
0.6
0.5
0.4
0.3
0.2
0.1
0.6M.   0.6 M.

METERS

SADDLE ROCK GRIST MILL

The Saddle Rock Grist Mill in Nassau County, Long Island, provides a good example of a tidemill. At high tide, water is retained behind a dam (at left in photo above). When the tide goes out, water trapped behind the dam drives the wheel; the photo below shows the higher level of water behind the dam at low tide, and the undershot wheel driven by this head of water. Photos: Nassau County Museum.

in Massachusetts. Governor John Winthrop built a mill in New London, Connecticut, which is still standing. Some indication of the way the colonists turned to power for their mills can be gleaned from the fact that by 1649 there were five watermills, four windmills, and numerous horse-powered mills in Virginia alone.

Time has changed the scene with an inexorable hand. There are left today few mills driven by flowing streams, the tides, or the wind. A few are in private hands and a few others have been restored and are maintained by government and privately financed institutions and foundations.

Philipsburg Manor:
The History

There is no established date for the arrival in what was then New Amsterdam of a Dutchman named Frederick Flypse, or Flypsen, who came to the New World as an employee of the Dutch West India Company and soon became Peter Stuyvesant's carpenter. Flypse, whose name frequently appeared in records spelled as "Philipse," was probably not just a man with a hammer and saw, but one with at least basic knowledge of architecture, construction, and other arts useful to a builder.

It is not until 1653 that the records specifically make mention of Flypse, noting that he acted as appraiser of a house and lot in the city. This would seem to indicate that the immigrant was more than Stuyvesant's carpenter. He was already something of an expert and an entrepreneur. In the next seven years Flypse, or Philipse, showed himself to be a man of no limited vision, for in September 1660, he was applying to the West India Company for a charter to operate one of the company's sloops to Virginia for purposes of trade. As the years passed, Philipse's interests expanded into real estate, commerce with other colonies, the West Indies, and the Old World, and many other forms of business enterprise. He owned warehouses, at least one ship of his own, chartered others, and began a steady accretion of valuable real estate at the tip of Manhattan.

Two years after seeking permission to charter a ship from the West India Company, he asked the local dominie to solemnize a marriage between himself and Margaret Hardenbroeck De Vries, a wealthy widow with a fleet of merchant ships of her own. This union provided more funds for expansion, and ten years later, with two business associates, Philipse purchased 7,700 acres of land just across the Harlem River at Spuyten Duyvil. This land had been included in the patroonship originally granted Adriaen van der Donck when the Dutch West India Company sought to colonize their holdings by giving vast parcels of land to stockholders who would bring fifty settlers over from Holland and set them up on his land.

With one exception, a vast holding at Albany called Rensselaerswyck, these patroonships failed. Philipse was just one of several businessmen in the little city on Manhattan who saw a chance to acquire vast real estate holdings at this time. Until he died many years later, he never ceased investing in residential plots in Manhattan and open land up the Hudson.

Philipse continued to acquire land. He bought out his two associates in the first big acquisition as soon as he could and then went on to purchase other huge plots. One of the first, strangely enough, was not contiguous to the initial purchase on the mainland above the city. It was a crescent-shaped parcel on both sides of the Pocantico River, obtained from the Indians. Soon afterward he filled in the area between and so owned all the land from Spuyten Duyvil to the Croton River. This property stretched inland at least a third of the way across Westchester County, as far as the meandering Bronx River.

If it appears this former carpenter for Stuyvesant spent all his time buying up land, the opposite is true. He was primarily a trader, with businesses in many ports and a deep-sea fleet to serve them. His ships plied the sea lanes to the West Indies, Europe, and the Indian Ocean. And his political career was as startlingly successful as his mercantile achievements. Governor Edmund Andros, the English administrator of what had become New York, named him an alderman, approved of his actions in that post, and then named him to the Governor's Council. By this time, Philipse had become the wealthiest man in the colony.

Frederick and Margaret had four children before she died. He remarried, again choosing a widow, Catharine Van Cortlandt Dervall, resulting in the linking of two famous families and two great fortunes.

It must have been a proud moment in Frederick's life when dignitaries handed him a royal patent or charter creating the "Lordship or Mannour of Philipsborough." The date was June 12, 1693, forty years after the first mention of his name in the annals of New Amsterdam and New York.

Frederick Philipse was not the sort of man to sit in the city and let fifty thousand acres of land upriver lie fallow. Everything in the Philipse world had to pay its way. Tenants sowed their seeds and built houses on Philipse's property, and two settlements were constructed along the river to serve as headquarters. Each was to have a gristmill, and each would be a commercial center, sending out flour and ship biscuit made from flour and importing trade goods and supplies needed for the tenants.

One was erected at Yonkers, in the southern reaches of the vast holding, near where the Nepperhan River flows into the Hudson. The other, known as the Upper Mills, was constructed where the Pocantico meets the Hudson, near presentday North Tarrytown.

An inquisitive visitor to Philipsburg Manor, Upper Mills, today can easily visualize why Frederick Philipse built his northern milling center there. If this visitor looks to the east, upriver from the millpond and dam, he will see beyond the modern highway bridge to where the river cuts through between two rock banks. He must imagine a larger flow of water in the Pocantico, as much of what normally fed that stream is now turned away into the water-supply system of neighboring communities.

In Philipse's time the Pocantico ran full and fast toward its junction with the Hudson. It had not silted up as it did when the New York Central tracks were built along its banks. By building a dam across the Pocantico, Philipse's workers created a fine millpond, with a good elevation above the mill's water wheel. Such an arrangement would provide for an overshot wheel—the most efficient kind. With the steady flow of water, the Pocantico would keep the riverbed

PHILIPSE MANOR HALL, YONKERS
This 18th century watercolor of Philipse Manor Hall in
Yonkers shows the site as it would have appeared when the
Philipses built their first manor house and gristmill there.
The drawing is dated "June 18, 1784" and marked "D. R.
fecit" but the artist is unidentified.

PHILIPSBURG MANOR, UPPER MILLS
The view across the millpond at Philipsburg Manor, Upper
Mills, shows the restored Manor House (right),
reconstructed gristmill (center) and bridge above the
mill dam.

clean and the broad-beamed sloops could easily make their way the short distance from the Hudson to the wharf built beside the mill. Thus the site offered fine water power for the mill and good navigation for transportation.

It was an ideal situation. A four-room stone house with a cellar below it, dug out of the bank of the pond, was erected, the mill on a stone-and-timber foundation put up nearby, and the dam built across the stream to form the pond.

There is no document showing exactly when the Upper Mills came into being, but there is one dated April 1, 1680, mentioning the granting of rights for "erecting and building a mill and making a damme" at Pocantico, and in 1684 the then Governor Dongan confirmed Frederick's title "to the Creeke Pocanteco or Weehkanteco upon which at present stands the mill of the sd. Frederick Philipse."

This evidence suggests that at least by 1684 Philipse was engaged in a commercial venture of great significance. Wheat raised by his tenants in the rich valleys of northern Westchester was being ground into flour at his Upper Mills, packed into barrels made in a cooperage shop near the mill, shipped by sloop from his wharf to New York City, where it was sifted or "bolted" at his own bolting mill on Manhattan. For several years, there was a law in existence forbidding the bolting of flour any place other than the city, but Frederick Philipse had vision. He could grind his flour on the Pocantico and sift it in Manhattan, keeping the profits firmly in his own hands.

But this was only a part of his commercial enter-

WHARF AT THE UPPER MILLS
Meal ground at the gristmill of Philipsburg Manor, Upper
Mills, was packed in barrels and shipped by sloop to New
York City for bolting. Drawing by Robert Fink.

prise, a model example of a full-scale production-distribution cycle, unique for its time. There was also a bake house at the Upper Mills, where some of the flour was baked into the hardtack called ship biscuit, a must for survival at sea before refrigeration or canning were mastered. Both flour and biscuit were sold in New York and to ships heading to sea, as well as supplying the Philipse merchant fleet itself.

Finally, in this economically sound venture, the existence of several hundred men, women, and children working or living near the mills provided a market for many items brought back to this country from Europe. There were furniture, spices, kitchen utensils, farm tools, cloth, notions, hardware, and other items that could not be easily manufactured in the New World, and trade goods suitable for swapping with the Indians for the rich pelts the European markets were crying for. These included cheap guns, hatchets, gay-colored cloth, beads, gimcracks, and clay tobacco pipes. Like many other New York merchants, Frederick Philipse was also involved in the slave trade.

That first mill may have been crude and rough, but it served Frederick well, as it did his son, Adolph, who enlarged and improved his father's holdings and interests. There was plenty of building material at hand, fieldstone for foundations and huge oaks for heavy timbers. The dam was fashioned of logs with a foundation of cribbing to hold rocks and clay. A footpath on its top gave the miller easy access to the floodgates.

Frederick Philipse was not content to have his northern headquarters be a purely commercial com-

ADOLPH PHILIPSE
Portrait of Adolph Philipse (1665–1750), second owner of
Philipsburg Manor, in oil on pine panel, c. 1695, by an
unknown artist. Courtesy of Museum of the City of
New York.

plex. His stout stone house served many purposes: kitchen for the hired hands, office for the manager, attic storeroom, but most important, a pleasant if simple dwelling for members of the family when there on business.

Although he was the wealthiest man in the colony at the time, Frederick's home was austere and plain. Thinking of the word "manor," one is apt to envision a splendid large mansion. The Philipse house was a solid oblong of stone and timber, almost like a blockhouse, with only four rooms and a basement kitchen for the servants.

Another indication of Frederick's concept of what his rural home should be can be gleaned from the fact that, almost as soon as he had completed the mill and house, he built a church which was, although not ornate, more imposing than his own home. Fieldstone was used in its construction, but so too were small bricks that may have come from the Netherlands.

Frederick Philipse had a bell cast in Holland for his church, and it bears the date 1685. What is more important, because it shows the character of this early entrepreneur, is the inscription it bears: SI DEUS PRO NOBIS QUIS CONTRA NOS (If God be for us, who can be against us?).

From the time the mill was completed, which was some time before 1684, until the outbreak of the Revolutionary War, the Upper Mills was a beehive of activity. Wagons and boats came in from fields stretching away from the Hudson as far as the Saw Mill River each autumn, laden with grain that was ground between the stones of the two mills powered by the single

OLD DUTCH CHURCH OF SLEEPY HOLLOW
Built during the 1680s, the old Dutch Church of Sleepy
Hollow still stands along U.S. Route 9, near the Manor
House and gristmill of the Upper Mills. In the adjacent
cemetery is the grave of Washington Irving, creator of such
memorable stories as "Rip Van Winkle" and "The Legend
of Sleepy Hollow." Photo: Budnik/Magnum.

water wheel. At first the flour and meal were shipped direct to the bolting house in Manhattan, but later, when the Bolting Act was rescinded, it was sifted under the same roof.

Broad-beamed sloops tied up to the wharf, or anchored in the safe estuary that the Dutch sailors, knowing its value as a haven from storms streaking across the Tappan Zee, called "die Slapering Haven." This old name appealed to Washington Irving who used it to denote the slumbering, drowsy neighborhood which he later called Sleepy Hollow. Slaves baked sea biscuit in the bake house, and tenants who had cut the staves during the off season constructed barrels to hold the flour.

Cattle browsed on the meadows behind the barn, chickens scratched in the barnyard, and ducks and geese swam on the millpond. The summer stillness was broken by the cries of boatmen casting off their lines for the voyage to New York, the splashing of the great water wheel, and the humming of bees in the woven-reed hives beyond the herb garden.

Frederick Philipse demonstrated his fondness for the Upper Mills by requesting in his will that his executors bury him in the graveyard of the church he had built—a church now known wherever Washington Irving's legends are read, as the Old Dutch Church of Sleepy Hollow.

Adolph Philipse was as devoted to the land and the Upper Mills as his father. Under his tutelage the commerical enterprise flourished, the trade routes expanded and the size of the manor house doubled by the simple expedient of adding rooms that duplicated those of the original. The tenant population exploded

TARRYTOWN
"Tarry Town where Major André was captured," a lithograph from Jacques Milbert's *Picturesque Itinerary of the Hudson River*, suggests the beauty and calm along the Hudson River in earlier days.

MANOR HOUSE AT PHILIPSBURG MANOR, UPPER MILLS
During the time of Adolph Philipse, the size of the original
Manor House was doubled by adding rooms which
duplicated those of the original.

from two hundred to eleven hundred before Adolph died in 1750.

The picture changed when the founder's son died. Ownership passed to Frederick Philipse II, a nephew who died before he could leave much of a mark. But his son, Frederick III, had little of the older Philipses' character and energy. Preferring to dwell in a family home in Yonkers, he rented out the Upper Mills within a year of his father's death. His principal activities focused on financial dealings in New York City; politically, he began to emerge as a Tory.

As the thirteen colonies moved further away from the mother country, and talk of independence was heard in legislature, church, home, and tavern, Frederick III opted to remain loyal to the Crown. He lived luxuriously, reaping the benefits of his great-grandfather's and his great-uncle's industry and vision. Finally, when the inevitable occurred and every man had to decide whether to be loyal to the Crown or loyal to a dream of independence and a nation built upon individual freedom, Frederick III chose the former.

Thinking to ride out the storm in his Yonkers mansion, the last Philipse to own the Upper Mills was arrested in 1776. Later he moved his family inside the British lines in Manhattan, remaining there until 1783 when he went to England, to die a bitter man, attainted of treason, with his lands put up for sale by Commissioners of Forfeiture.

Gerard G. Beekman, Jr., a New York businessman, bought the Upper Mills portion of the manor, amounting to 750 acres. Much of the balance of the estate was cut up into parcels as small as a single acre

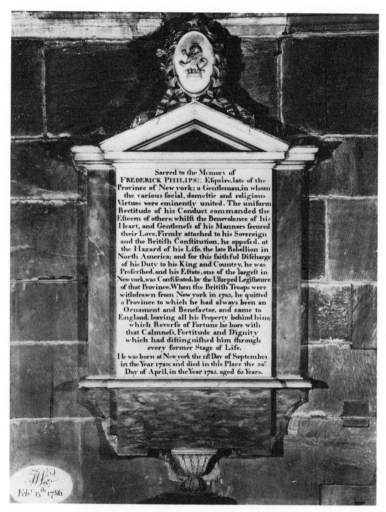

Sacred to the Memory of
FREDERICK PHILIPSE Esquire, late of the
Province of New york; a Gentleman, in whom
the various social, domestic and religious
Virtues were eminently united. The uniform
Rectitude of his Conduct commanded the
Esteem of others; whilst the Benevolence of his
Heart, and Gentleness of his Manners secured
their Love, Firmly attached to his Sovereign
and the British Constitution, he opposed, at
the Hazard of his Life, the late Rebellion in
North America; and for this faithful Discharge
of his Duty to his King and Country, he was
Proscribed, and his Estate, one of the largest in
New york, was Confiscated, by the Usurped Legislature
of that Province. When the British Troops were
withdrawn from New york in 1783, he quitted
a Province to which he had always been an
Ornament and Benefactor, and came to
England, leaving all his Property behind him;
which Reverse of Fortune he bore with
that Calmness, Fortitude and Dignity
which had distinguished him through
every former Stage of Life.
He was born at New york the 1st Day of September
in the Year 1720; and died in this Place the 30th
Day of April, in the Year 1785, aged 65 Years.

Feb 15th 1786.

FREDERICK PHILIPSE'S CRYPT MARKER

Frederick Philipse III, a Loyalist, fled to England after the
American Revolution, and died in Chester, where he is
buried in the graveyard of the Chester Cathedral.

and when all was sold 287 different individuals owned the empire that had been created and run by the first two Philipses.

Gerard Beekman operated the Upper Mills until his death in 1822, but it was a sporadic enterprise. His widow, Cornelia, a great-grandniece of Catharine, second wife of the first Frederick Philipse, decided to divide the estate, some parcels going for building lots in the mushrooming village.

The property passed through many hands. The last private owner was Miss Elsie Janis, the famous singer who entertained so many doughboys during World War I and who was known as "The Sweetheart of the AEF." Unable to pay for its upkeep, Miss Janis lost the property in the Depression, a bank foreclosing the mortgage in 1937. From the time when Frederick Philipse bought it from the Indians, it had been in private hands for two and a half centuries.

Aware of the great historic value of the Upper Mills, even though the house had been altered beyond recognition and the mills that had replaced the original one had fallen into decay, the Historical Society of the Tarrytowns undertook to preserve the sadly diminished holding for the public. Enlisting the financial aid and active encouragement of one of its most renowned neighbors, Mr. John D. Rockefeller, Jr., the Society purchased the Upper Mills. Later it passed into the hands of Sleepy Hollow Restorations, the educational organization set up by Mr. Rockefeller to restore and maintain not only the Upper Mills, but Van Cortlandt Manor in Croton-on-Hudson, and Washington Irving's home, Sunnyside, in Tarrytown.

PHILIPSBURG MANOR HOUSE, C. 1918
Over the years, many additions were made to the original
Manor House at Philipsburg Manor, Upper Mills. This
photograph, c. 1918, shows the house as it appeared during
the ownership of Elsie Janis.

VAN CORTLANDT MANOR AND SUNNYSIDE
Sleepy Hollow Restorations, which maintains Philipsburg
Manor, Upper Mills, also owns and operates Van Cortlandt
Manor (above) in Croton-on-Hudson, N.Y., and Sunnyside
(next page) in Tarrytown, N.Y.

Time and events had not been kind to the vast manorial holdings of the Philipses. Little by little the fifty thousand acres had been sold off, nibbled away, or cut adrift in other ways. The redeeming feature of it all was that the very nexus of that huge empire—the site of the gristmill, millpond, dam, and manor house was still intact. With the twenty acres of land on which they stood, one of the unique and historic properties in America could be restored to the condition it was in when it was at the peak of its importance.

It was now up to the genius of architects, contractors, archeologists, historians, and others to put the pieces together again.

Philipsburg Manor, Upper Mills:
Today

The restoration and reconstruction of Philipsburg Manor, Upper Mills, was a difficult task. First of all, there was a lack of precise documentation as to location and appearance of the original mill itself. No artist had sketched the Philipse mill, or at least no picture was known to exist. There is no record as to the mill's earliest appearance; changes had always been made as repairs became necessary.

During the War for Independence, the Pocantico was practically in the middle of a considerable territory between the British lines in southern Westchester and the patriot lines in northern Westchester. This area, called "the neutral ground," was infested with guerrillas and lawless irregulars known as Skinners and Cowboys. While professing to support one or the other of the belligerents, they spent the bulk of their time looting and burning the properties abandoned by owners who had fled to safety within the British or American lines.

What actual harm was done to the Philipse mill is not known, but records of Van Cortlandt Manor, eight miles or so up the river, show that the house was vandalized, so there is every reason to believe the Philipse mill also was extensively damaged. Yet repairs must have been made, for the Beekman mill book, a record of work done under the new owner's control, shows milling operations continued into the years 1795, 1796, and 1797.

From the last year to 1839, there is no record of steady milling activities at the mouth of the Pocantico. These years correspond generally with a period during which a wheat blight struck throughout the eastern states. Activity elsewhere picked up after 1830 when a blight-free strain was introduced from Belgium, but the Philipse mill, or what was left of it, fell into such disuse that Beekman's will in 1822 did not even mention it, although referring to many other buildings and structures. Obviously Gerard Beekman had allowed the mill to fall into complete disrepair.

Just when it appeared that milling was abandoned on the old Philipse estate, the *Hudson River Chronicle*, under date of February, 1839, carried an advertisement stating that the mill had been "put in the most very best state of repair, with the addition of the latest and most improved machinery for cleaning the grain, with three run of stones and new bolters."

There is a map in existence, published in 1848, entitled *Map of the Beekman Farm situated in the Town of Mount Pleasant*, which clearly shows the gristmill, dam, and millpond. Little more is known about the mill until 1910, when it was demolished after a tree fell on it.

There the matter stood until the Historical Society of the Tarrytowns rescued the surviving acreage and manor house with the financial assistance of Mr. Rock-efeller. A mill was reconstructed in 1941, and the public could once again see what milling was like in colonial days. After Sleepy Hollow Restorations took control of the property in 1951, it was determined that more thorough research should be undertaken to establish the true dimensions of the Philipse mill and then to reconstruct such a mill on the precise site of Frederick Philipse's original building. Once this decision had been made, it was necessary to tear down the 1941 mill, remove its foundations, and search for the remains of a building that had been erected more than two and a half centuries before.

A team of experienced men and women was organized, including architects, archeologists, researchers, and millwrights. All known records dealing with the Philipses, Beekmans, and other tenants, tax and real estate transfer documents, and old newspapers were studied for mention of the activities and structures at the Upper Mills. Other colonial mills—the few in existence—were examined and studied for structural details.

Once the 1941 mill was torn down, the ground in the vicinity of the manor house, mill, wharf, and environs was marked off into grids, each section numbered, and archeological digging commenced. Under the foundations of the 1941 mill were found the foundations of an earlier structure, which measurements revealed was the one illustrated on the 1848 map, also shown in paintings done by unknown artists about 1850 as well as a Currier and Ives print of 1865.

A coffer dam was erected to keep out the water

EXCAVATIONS AT PHILIPSBURG MANOR, UPPER MILLS
Archaeological excavations at Philipsburg Manor, Upper Mills, uncovered the site and remains of the original mill (above, center) and dam (above, upper left). Below is a closer view of the work on excavations of the mill dam. Photo: W. W. Hennessy.

PHILIPSBURG MANOR, UPPER MILLS, C. 1850
This oil painting by an unknown artist depicts the
appearance of Philipsburg Manor, Upper Mills, c. 1850.

and this remnant of the so-called Beekman mill was then removed. As digging continued, stone foundations of a still earlier mill and dam were distinterred, together with rotted timbers of the dam and rows of sapling piles upon which the earliest dry stone foundations of the Philipse mill were supported in the peat of the riverbed. Architects, studying the remaining timbers of the dam, noted several different techniques used in joining the wooden pieces, indicating that storms and floods had more than once washed out portions of the earliest dam, requiring repairs.

Meanwhile the digging of the various grid sections turned up a host of shards and ancient artifacts. They included eighteenth- and nineteenth-century ceramics, stoneware, red and yellow bricks similar to those brought from Holland, delftware, glass, clay tobacco pipes, iron spikes and nails, wooden gears, and a water wheel shaft. Some of these items were parts used in the mill, some the discarded refuse of daily living.

All this digging established beyond any doubt how large the Philipse mill had been and precisely where it had stood. With this information in hand, architects, builders, and millwrights went to work to erect a replica. In the terms of historians and architects, the mill is a reconstruction. This means that there was insufficient material on which to rebuild or to add construction. But the research had established what the original mill was like, where it was located, and how it was built. The one now operating at Philipsburg Manor is therefore a reconstruction: as accurate a replica as study and research can make it.

On the other hand, the manor house is a restora-

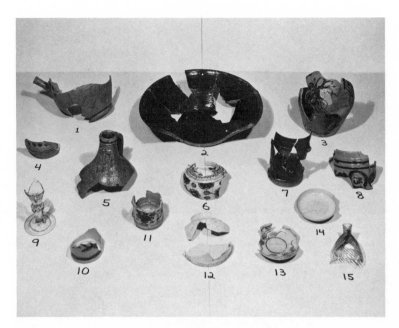

ARTIFACTS UNCOVERED AT PHILIPSBURG MANOR, UPPER MILLS

Artifacts of many kinds were uncovered in the
archaeological excavations at Philipsburg Manor,
Upper Mills.

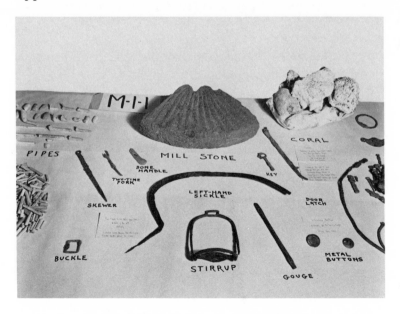

CLAY PIPE FRAGMENTS
Large numbers of clay pipe fragments were found during
the archaeological digging.

RECONSTRUCTION OF THE MILL

The gristmill which presently stands at Philipsburg Manor, Upper Mills, is a reconstruction which attempts to duplicate as nearly as possible the nature, appearance, and location of the original mill. Above is a photograph of workmen beginning the early stages of reconstruction of the mill and dam. Photographs on the following page show later stages of the reconstruction, with the mill nearing completion.

Skilled craftsmen carefully reconstructed the mill at
Philipsburg Manor, Upper Mills, a working gristmill of the
type built during the eighteenth century.

tion. Although altered here and there, and added to by many tenants after Adolph Philipse died, the researchers were able to identify clearly the basic stone walls of the two-room, attic, and kitchen-below house built by Frederick, and the identical addition joined to it by Adolph. These walls had been changed but little, mostly for enlarged window openings. Huge timbers from the original house were still intact in some of the flooring and even more in the roof supports.

As the late additions were removed from the stout, squarely built stone structure that existed at the peak of the Upper Mills' activity, one could easily see the line where Adolph's enlargement was joined to the earlier house. This line, running up and down the walls in front and rear of the manor house, is easily noticeable to even the youngest of visitors.

It required ten years to remove the 1941 mill, study the artifacts found in the earth near the mill and manor house, conduct the research necessary for planning a reconstruction, and build the mill precisely as it would have been done around the first decades of the eighteenth century.

Existing mills in this country and in Europe, some of them built at the same time the Philipse mill was erected, were studied, as were old manuals and books used by millwrights. As a result of this research, construction methods used in the mid-twentieth century for the reconstruction were as close to those of the Philipse workmen as study and historical knowledge could establish. Timbers were joined as craftsmen had joined them in colonial days, nails and other hardware were hand-made by blacksmiths, and the dam built

MANOR HOUSE AT PHILIPSBURG MANOR, UPPER MILLS
Visitors approaching the Manor House as they cross the
bridge over the mill dam can easily see the central dividing
line in the house where Adolph Philipse duplicated the
original rooms to enlarge the structure.

across the Pocantico in the same way the elder Philipse had had it done.

There is only one major difference between today's reconstruction and the first mill and dam. This was made necessary by the alteration in the stream's flow when water was deflected into a local reservoir system. If the river had been dammed sufficiently to produce a head of water for an overshot wheel, the pond behind the dam would have interfered with today's bridges, highways, and other structures. Therefore, a low breastwheel arrangement was substituted for the original overshot wheel.

Out of sight, beneath the dam, are hidden concrete and steel structures to prevent undermining, and valves to permit draining of the pond. Naturally, they comply with modern safety practices required by law, but they are not visible, and in no way harm the appearance of the restoration of the Upper Mills.

Today's mill can easily turn out two tons of flour or cornmeal a day, just as a colonial counterpart could have in the days of Frederick and Adolph Philipse. Few devices perfected in the years before the Revolutionary War were as efficient and no other could work under the supervision of but a single man.

As the nation moved through the Industrial Revolution and into the age of modern technology, the gristmill became obsolete, but it never lost its romantic appeal. The mill at Philipsburg Manor is one of a few still operating, one of the few that modern man can study and marvel at.

Across the span of centuries the miller changed but little. His character, it seems, was influenced by the

THE MILLER EXPLAINS HIS CRAFT
An expert on mills and milling, Charles Howell is always
willing to share his extensive knowledge with visitors to
Philipsburg Manor, Upper Mills.

sober nature of the milling process itself. Literature has given us many descriptions of millers—many of them jolly, warm-hearted men, important members of their communities, perhaps a little wide of girth compared to farmers, blacksmiths, and sawyers, but generally well content with their lot.

In both war and peace the miller was a favorite resident, full of gossip and news brought from far and near to the gristmill along with the grain to be ground. Many an early housewife must have envied her husband the privilege of sitting and chatting with the miller as the great water wheel splashed, the stones rotated, and the damsel clattered.

The millers who operated the mill for Frederick and Adolph Philipse must have enjoyed many benefits from their bucolic life. They could see flocks of Canada geese resting on the millpond during Spring and Fall migrations, watch mallards teaching their young to swim in the placid waters below the millrace, where the water, turned to froth by the wheel, quieted down again, and marvel at barn swallows foraging for insects to carry back to mud-wattled nests appliquéd to rafters above stables and stalls.

They knew the excitement of exchanging words with Hudson River sloop sailors who had been to the city and perhaps to foreign ports, with tenants and Indians and soldiers. And they surely knew the peace that came at eventide, when the wheel was still and there was only the sound of water falling over the spillway of the dam.

CANADA GEESE AT THE MILLPOND
Migrating Canada geese still stop to rest at the millpond of
Philipsburg Manor, Upper Mills, where a piece of history is
kept alive.

For Further Reading

Bathe, Grenville and Dorothy Bathe. *Oliver Evans: A Chronicle of Early American Engineering.* Philadelphia: Historical Society of Pennsylvania, 1935.

Bennett, Richard and John Elton. *History of Corn Milling,* 4 vols. New York: Burt Franklin, 1964 (reprint of 1904 edition).

Brangwyn, Frank and Hayter Preston. *Windmills.* Detroit: Gale Research Co., 1975 (reprint of 1923 edition).

Evans, Oliver. *The Young Mill-wright and Miller's Guide.* Philadelphia, 1836; reprinted New York: Arno Press, 1972.

Freese, Stanley. *Windmills and Millwrighting.* Cranbury, N.J.: A. S. Barnes & Co., 1972.

Gray, Andrew. *The Experienced Millwright.* Edinburgh, 1804.

Hamilton, Edward P. *The Village Mill in Early New England.* Sturbridge, Mass., 1964

Hindle, Brooke, ed. *America's Wooden Age: Aspects of Its Early Technology.* Tarrytown; N.Y.: Sleepy Hollow Restorations, 1975.

Howell, Kenneth T. *Empire Over the Dam.* Chester, Conn.: Pequot Press, 1974.

Hughes, William Carter. *The American Miller and Millwrights' Assistant.* Detroit: Harsha and Hart, 1850.

Jaray, Cornell, comp. *The Mills of Long Island.* Port Washington, N.Y.: I. J. Friedman, 1962.

Jesperson, Anders. *Mills and Their Preservation.* Copenhagen, 1963.

————. *Preliminary Analysis of the Development of the Gearing in Watermills in Western Europe.* Virum, Denmark, 1953.

Kuhlman, Charles B. *Development of the Flour Milling Industry in the United States.* Clifton, N.J.: Augustus M. Kelley, 1968 (reprint of 1929 edition).

Magee, Henry. *The Miller in Eighteenth Century Virginia.* Williamsburg, Va.: Colonial Williamsburg Foundation, 1958.

Rawson, Marion L. *Little Old Mills.* New York: E. P. Dutton & Co., 1935; reprinted New York: Johnson Reprint Corp., 1970.

Reynolds, John. *Windmills and Watermills.* New York: Praeger, 1970.

Skilton, C. P. *British Windmills and Watermills.* London: Collins, 1947.

Steen, Herman. *Flour Milling in America.* Westport, Conn.: Greenwood Press, 1973 (reprint of 1963 edition).

Swanson, Leslie C. *Old Mills in the Midwest.* Moline, Ill.: Swanson, 1963.

Torrey, Volta. *Wind-Catchers: American Windmills of Yesterday and Tomorrow.* Brattleboro, Vt.: Stephen Greene Press, 1976.

Wailes, Rex. *The English Windmill.* London: Routledge, 1954; reprinted 1976.

Walton, J. *Water-Mills, Windmills and Horse-Mills of South Africa.* Mystic, Conn.: Lawrence Verry, 1974.

Weiss, Harry B. and Grace M. Zeigler. *Early Fulling Mills of New Jersey.* Trenton: New Jersey Agricultural Society, 1957.

Weiss, Harry B. and Robert J. Sim. *Early Grist and Flouring Mills of New Jersey.* Trenton: New Jersey Agricultural Society, 1956.

Weiss, Harry B. and Grace M. Ziegler. *Early Sawmills of New Jersey.* Trenton: New Jersey Agricultural Society, 1968.

Weiss, Harry B. and Grace M. Weiss. *Early Windmills of New Jersey and Nearby States.* Trenton: New Jersey Agricultural Society, 1969.

Wilson, Paul N. *Watermills with Horizontal Wheels.* Kendal, England: Titus Wilson & Son, Ltd., 1960.

Zimiles, Martha and Murray Zimiles. *Early American Mills.* New York: Clarkson N. Potter, 1973.

Glossary

apron — arc of stone or wood placed behind a pitchback
or breastshot water wheel to prevent water from
spilling from the buckets of the wheel before
arriving at the lowest point of the fall

arms — spokes extending from the main shaft of a
water wheel, which in turn support the shrouding or rims of the wheel; or spokes of a large
gear wheel

bails — large iron tongs suspended from a crane, used
to lift off the upper stone of a pair for dressing
or other adjustments to the stones (see illustration, p. 84)

balance rynd — curved iron bar which crosses the eye of
the runner stone, fitting into slots on either
side — also called *millstone bridge* or *crossbar* —
also see *rynd*

bed stone — lower, stationary stone in a pair of
millstones

"big" wheel — see *master face wheel*

bill — see *mill bill*

bill thrift — wooden handle with a slotted or morticed
top into which a mill bill can be fitted for use

bins — storage containers for grain, usually on the

upper floor of a mill, from which grain could be fed into millstone hoppers—also called *garners*

bist—cushion, usually made of a partly-filled sack of meal or bran, used by a worker when dressing millstones

blades—in general, panels attached to a shaft to harness water or wind power—also used to refer specifically to the panels attached to the spindle of the early Greek-type watermill—also called *vanes*

Blue stones—see *Cullin stones*

bolter—machine used to sift flour into lots of differing textures or degrees of fineness

bolting cloth—cloth of varying weave used to sift flour into lots according to texture; sometimes made of silk, and thus often called "*silks*"

bran—outer coating of a grain of wheat

brayer—linkage connecting *tentering staff* and *bridgetree*

breastshot wheel—water wheel powered by a head of water striking the wheel at a point from one-third to two-thirds the height of the wheel, causing the wheel to revolve in a direction opposite to that of the flow of water in the sluiceway (see illustration, p. 40)

bridgetree—adjustable beam upon which the millstone spindle is supported; may be raised or lowered to alter the distance between the grinding surfaces of the stones in order to produce a finer or coarser meal—also see *tentering staff*

bridging box—housing, mounted on the bridgetree, which contains footstep bearing supporting the millstone spindle and ensuring that the spindle will run perfectly upright—also called *tram pot*

buckets—blades, or enclosures formed by blades, around the rim of a water wheel, against which or into which water flows in order to turn the wheel—also see *floats*

bucket wheel—water wheel using an enclosed bucket, rather than a simple blade or float, to harness water power

butterfly furrow—the smallest of four furrows in one quarter of a millstone in quarter dress—also called *fly furrow*

cant—segment of one of the rings which form the rim of a water wheel or wooden gear wheel

cap—rotating top of a tower or smock windmill

casing—see *stone case*

circular furrow dress—see *sickle dress*

cockeye—socket at center of balance rynd, which serves as supporting bearing for the runner stone

cock head—pivot point at top of millstone spindle, which fits into the cockeye

Cologne stones—see *Cullin stones*

conical quern—quern composed of two conical-shaped stones, the top portion of the upper stone being hopper-shaped for feeding grain between the grinding surfaces—also called *hourglass mill* (see illustration, p. 21)

control gate—gate at the end of the flume nearest the water wheel, used to control the flow of water from the flume to the wheel—also called *shut*

counter-gearing (counter gears)—system of two-step

gearing using a combination of face or spur gears and wallowers to drive millstone spindles (see illustration, p. 63)

cracks—fine lines cut into the face of a millstone in the areas between furrows

crossbar—see *balance rynd*

crotch—device placed at the lower end of the quant or millstone spindle in overdrift drive, engaging the rynd and thus driving the runner stone—shaped like the crotch in a pair of slacks, or a fork in the road, hence also called a *forked end*

Cullin stones—German millstones of dark bluish-gray lava with even pores—the name is derived from a corruption of Köln, the German name for the city called Cologne in English—the stones are also known as *Blue stones, Cologne stones, Holland stones,* or *Rhine stones*

curb—track on which the cap of a tower or smock windmill turns

damsel—square shaft, squared section of a rounded shaft, or forked iron shaft fit over the top of the millstone spindle, which in rotating taps against the shoe, thus feeding grain into the stones

draft—the radius of the draft circle

draft circle—an imaginary circle around the eye of a millstone, from which master furrows radiate tangentially

drawing out—process by which mill bills are thinned out at their chisel ends

dress—the layout or pattern of furrows on a millstone —also used with respect to flour to mean "sift" *dressing*—the process of cutting grooves (cracks or furrows) into the face of a millstone, in order to provide a shearing action in grinding, or sharpening the existing dress—also called *facing*

driver—cast iron bar fitted onto the millstone spindle; the ends of the driver fit into slots in the eye of the runner stone and thus connect the runner stone to the spindle

drum boards—see *sole*

Esopus stones—millstones produced by the Esopus Millstone Company, composed of Shawangunk Conglomerate Grit

eye—central hole in a millstone

eye staff—a shorter type of paint staff, usually about two feet in length, used to test the surface of the millstone around the eye

face gear (face wheel)—wheel with cogs morticed into its face, usually used in conjunction with a lantern pinion

facing—usually, dressing around the eye section of millstones—also see *dressing*

facing hammer—tool resembling a multiple-edged chisel, used for dressing or facing a millstone (see illustration, p. 83)

fall (of water)—see *head (of water)*

fantail—small vaned wind wheel set at right angles to the sails of a windmill, and connected to a gearing mechanism by means of which the sails are automatically kept square to the wind—also called *fly*

feather edge —grinding edge at the top of a tapered furrow

flume —trough or channel which carries water from the headrace to the point where the water strikes or enters the water wheel—also called *sluiceway* or *lade*

flume gate —gate at the end of the flume nearest the headrace or millpond, used to control the flow of water entering the flume—also called *sluice gate* —sometimes used interchangably with *control gate* or *shut*

fly —see *fantail*

fly furrow —see *butterfly furrow*

footstep bearing —thrust bearing, housed in bridging box, which supports the millstone spindle atop the bridgetree, or the bottom bearing of an upright shaft

forked end —see *crotch*

French burr (buhr) stones —millstones composed of separate pieces of freshwater quartz, each piece known as a burr, quarried in northern France

furrow —groove cut into the grinding surface of a millstone

garners —see *bins*

glut box —housing for the top bearing of the quant in overdrift drive

governor —regulator mechanism, usually centrifugal, used to maintain a preset distance between millstones in a windmill, and also in watermills when a varying head presents problems of speed control *great spur wheel*—spur gear used to transfer power from the main vertical spindle through lantern or spur pinions to millstone spindles in the form of two-step gearing known as spur gear drive (see illustration, p. 64)

Greek mill—simple, early form of horizontal mill, in which a horizontal water wheel with spoon-shaped blades is attached to the millstone spindle and drives the runner stone directly, without requiring any gearing

Grey stones—see *Peak stones*

gristmill—mill used for the grinding of grain, principally wheat or corn

gudgeon—metal journal mounted in the end of the main shaft to run in bearings (see illustration, p. 34)

head (of water)—the difference in level between water entering the water wheel and that leaving the wheel—also called *fall (of water)*

head water—water entering or feeding the water wheel

headrace—channel which conveys water from the dam or millpond to the flume or directly to the water wheel

Holland stones—see *Cullin stones*

hoop—see *stone case*

hopper—open-topped container tapered to feed grain to millstones

hopper ladder—see *horse*

horizontal mill—watermill whose wheel revolves in a horizontal plane—also see *Greek mill, Norse mill*

horse—wooden framework on top of stone case which

holds hopper in position—also called *hopper ladder*

hourglass mill—see *conical quern*

hub—center of water wheel, into which blades are morticed in a horizontal mill

hunting cog—cog inserted in gearing system to avoid simple gear ratios and thereby avert potential uneven wear due to inequalities in repeatedly meeting gear faces

husk—see *stone case*

jack stick—see *quill stick*

journeyman furrow—second largest furrow in a quarter of a millstone in quarter dress, parallel and immediately adjacent to the master furrow on one side and the prentice furrow on the other side (see illustration, p. 53)

lade—see *flume*

lands—areas between furrows on the grinding surface of a millstone

lantern pinion—pinion gear consisting of round staves morticed between two discs, used either as a *wallower* (see illustration, p. 52), or as a *millstone pinion* or *nut*

lay-shaft—shaft set at right angles to master face wheel which transfers drive to little face wheel in counter-gearing, or parallel driven shaft when master wheel is a spur gear wheel

little face wheel—face wheel which transfers drive from lay-shaft to millstone spindles in counter-gearing *mace*—device used to connect the quant or millstone spindle to the runner stone in overdrift; similar to the driver in underdrift drive

master face wheel—face wheel mounted on water wheel shaft in counter-gearing; used to transfer power to lay-shafts via lantern pinions—also called the *"big" wheel*

master furrow—largest furrow in a quarter of a millstone in quarter dress, determining the boundary of the quarter (see illustration, p. 53)

middlings—the coarsest part of the wheat meal ground by a mill; the last product excepting the bran remaining after finer grades of flour are sifted out in the bolting process—also called *sharps, shorts*

mill bill—chisel-ended tool used for dressing or sharpening the grinding surfaces of a millstone—also called *mill chisel*

mill chisel—see *mill bill*

mill peck—similar to *mill bill*, but with pointed ends—also called a *pritchell* or *mill pick*

mill pick—see *mill peck*

miller's toll—portion of ground meal retained by the miller as payment for his services; in the United States, usually ten to twenty per cent of the meal ground; in England, usually one-sixteenth

millpond—body of water, usually created by the construction of a dam, which serves as a source of water for the water wheel

millstone bridge—see *balance rynd*

Millstone Grit—name given by British millers to rock quarried in Yorkshire and Derbyshire, England, used in making Peak or Grey millstones

millstone pinion —see *nut*

mortar and pestle —simple grinding apparatus in which a receptacle (mortar) is used to hold grain while it is crushed by a club-shaped implement (pestle)

neck bearing —wooden bearing in center of bed stone, through which millstone spindle passes; or bearing supporting the front journal of the windshaft in a windmill

Norse mill —horizontal mill similar to Greek mill, but with straight inclined blades to facilitate the removal of ice in winter

nut —pinion, located at the top of the quant, which engages the great spur wheel in overdrift drive; or pinion mounted on the stone spindle in underdrift drive,—also called *millstone pinion, stone pinion*

overdrift drive —method of driving or turning millstones by bringing power down from above by means of a quant or millstone spindle connected from above to the runner stone

overshot wheel —water wheel powered by a head of water striking the wheel just forward of its highest point, causing the wheel to revolve in the same direction as the flow of water in the sluiceway (see illustration, p. 36)

paint staff —straight wooden staff to which a marking paint ("raddle" or "tiver") is applied; used to test for level surface on millstones *pair (of stones)* —set of two millstones, consisting of the upper or runner stone and the lower or bed stone—also called a *run (of stones)*

pan —cast-iron housing for bed stone, often found in late nineteenth-century mills

Peak stones —millstones produced from rock commonly called Millstone Grit quarried in the Peak District of southwest Yorkshire and northeast Derbyshire in England—also called *Grey stones*

peck —see *mill peck*

pick —see *mill peck*

pinion —see *lantern pinion, nut*

pit wheel —large face gear wheel mounted on the water wheel shaft

pitchback wheel —water wheel powered by a head of water striking the wheel at or just back of its highest point, causing the wheel to revolve in a direction opposite to that of the flow of water in the sluiceway (see illustration, p. 38)

pritchell —see *mill peck*

quant —shaft which serves as millstone spindle in overdrift drive

quarter —section of the surface of a millstone defined by master furrows; not necessarily one-fourth the surface area of the stone

quarter dress —form of millstone dress using a series of straight furrows, the largest of which divide the surface of the millstone into regions called "quarters" (see illustration, p. 78)

quern —simple form of rotary gristmill, consisting of a stationary lower stone and an upper stone usu-

ally rotated by hand with the aid of a stick or
lever fastened to the upper stone (see illustration, p. 19)

quill stick—flat piece of wood with hole to accommodate quill in one end, used to test millstone
spindle for true, upright running—also called
jack stick, tram stick (see illustration, p. 60)

raddle—mixture of red oxide powder and water, used
on a paint staff—also called *tiver*

rap—block on shoe against which the damsel strikes to
ensure an even flow of grain from the hopper to
the millstones

Rhine stones—see *Cullin stones*

rim—see shroud

run (of stones)—see *pair (of stones)*

runner stone—upper, moving stone in a pair of
millstones

rynd (rind)—crossbar containing the bearing on which
the upper stone of a pair of millstones rests

saddle-stone mill—simple grinding apparatus in which
meal is ground between a saddle-shaped stone
and a rounded stone which is rolled over it (see
illustration, p. 16)

sails—blades used to harness wind power in a windmill

sapling mill—form of plumping mill in which the resiliency of a sapling is used as an aid to driving a
mortar and pestle (see illustration, p. 28)

secondary furrows—furrows shorter than and running
parallel to master furrows in quarter dress

sharps—see *middlings*

shoe—tapering trough vibrated to feed grain into the
stones for grinding

shorts—see *middlings*

shroud (shrouding)—rim of water wheel, which forms
sides of bucket enclosures

shut—see *control gate*

sickle dress—form of millstone dress using a series of
semi-circular furrows of the same radius as the
millstone—also called *circular furrow dress* (see
illustration, p. 78)

silks—see *bolting cloth*

skirt—outer edge of the grinding surface of a
millstone

slip cog—removable cog in a pinion gear

sluice gate—see *flume gate*—sometimes used inter-
changeably with *shut*

sluiceway—see *flume*

smock mill—windmill, usually with octagonal timber
tower, giving something of the appearance of a
man wearing a smock

sole (soling)—inner lining of water wheel, forming bottom of bucket—also called *drum boards, sole
boards*

spindle—shaft on which runner stone rotates

spur gear (spur wheel)—gear with cogs morticed or cut
into its edge

spur gear drive—system of two-step gearing using a
system of face gears, spur gears, and lantern or
spur pinions to drive millstone spindles (see
illustration, p. 64)

starts—short spurs or arms projecting from the rim of
a water wheel, to which floats are fastened

stone case—circular wooden enclosure around a pair of millstones—also called *casing, hoop, husk, tun, vat* (see illustration, p. 90)

stone nut—see *nut*

stone pinion—see *nut*

sweep—staff connecting mortar to box which fills with water in a water-driven plumping mill (see illustration, p. 28)

sweeper—device attached to runner stone which sweeps meal from between the edges of the stones and the stone case and carries the meal to the spout opening in the case

tail water—water leaving the water wheel

tailrace—channel which conveys water from the water wheel back to the millstream

tentering—process of adjusting the distance between the upper and lower millstones—also see *tentering staff*

tentering staff—beam, connected to the bridgetree by the brayer, permitting the bridgetree to be raised or lowered and thus adjusting the distance between the upper and lower millstones

tide mill—watermill harnessing energy from tidal water which floods basins or river valleys at high tide (see illustration, p. 125)

tiver—see *raddle*

tower mill—windmill, usually round and built of stone or brick, with its gearing and millstones in a fixed tower with a rotating roof, or cap, containing the windshaft on which the sails are mounted *tram pot*—see *bridging box*

tram stick—see *quill stick*

trundle—lantern pinion on millstone spindle in counter-gearing; or a pinion resembling a smaller version of a face gear

tub mill—watermill with horizontal wheel enclosed to its full depth in a wooden casing

tun—see *stone case*

two-step gearing (two-step gear train)—systems of interlocking gears designed to permit several pairs of millstones to be driven from a single water wheel—see *counter-gearing, spur gear drive*

underdrift drive—method of driving or turning millstones by bringing power up from below by means of a millstone spindle connected from below to the runner stone through the eye of the bed stone

undershot wheel—water wheel powered by a head of water striking the wheel at a point near the bottom of the wheel, causing the wheel to revolve in a direction opposite to that of the flow of water in the sluiceway (see illustration, p. 43)

vanes—see *blades*

vat—see *stone case*

wallower—the first driven gear wheel in a water or wind mill, driven by gear wheel from main water wheel or windshaft

wind shaft—shaft on which sails are mounted in a
     windmill
winding—turning windmill sails into the wind

Index

About the Authors

CHARLES HOWELL is the resident Millwright and Master Miller of Philipsburg Manor, Upper Mills. He represents the fifth generation of a family of British millers, and has worked as a miller since the age of fourteen. He has supervised and consulted on the restoration and reconstruction of numerous mills in the United States and England and is a member of the British and North American Newcomen Societies, the Early American Industries Association, the Society for Industrial Archaeology, the Society for the History of Technology, and the Society for the Preservation of Old Mills.

ALLAN KELLER, formerly a featured columnist of the *New York World-Telegram and Sun* and professor of journalism at Columbia University, is a widely-published author. His previous works include *Colonial America, The Spanish-American War, Thunder at Harper's Ferry,* and, most recently, *Life Along the Hudson*, published in 1976 by Sleepy Hollow Restorations.

REX WAILES is an internationally renowned expert on mills and milling. He is the author of *The English Windmill* and of articles on windmills and water wheels in the *Encyclopaedia Brittanica*, and has been awarded numerous professional honors, including the Order of the British Empire and designation as a Fellow of the Society of Antiquaries of London, honorary Fellow of the Finnish Society of Antiquaries, Fellow of the Institution of Mechanical Engineers, and honorary Life Member of the International Molinological Society and the Newcomen Society of North America.

Sleepy Hollow Restorations, Incorporated, is a non-profit educational institution chartered by the *Board of Regents of the University of the State of New York*. Established under an endowment provided, in large part, by the late John D. Rockefeller, Jr., Sleepy Hollow Restorations owns and maintains *Sunnyside*, Washington Irving's picturesque home in Tarrytown; *Philipsburg Manor, Upper Mills*, in North Tarrytown, an impressive example of a colonial commercial mill complex; and *Van Cortlandt Manor*, in Croton-on-Hudson, a distinguished eighteenth-century family estate.